Skeet
and how to shoot it

BY

BOB NICHOLS

Skeet and Shooting Editor
Field and Stream

NEW YORK
GREENBERG : PUBLISHER

MANUFACTURED IN THE UNITED STATES OF AMERICA
BY THE VAIL-BALLOU PRESS, INC., BINGHAMTON, N. Y.

Courtesy of Grant Fitch

Got to miss some—and the station 2 outgoer is as good a place to miss as any.

CONTENTS

LIST OF ILLUSTRATIONS

LIST OF ILLUSTRATIONS

INTRODUCTION

A NEW word has come into the English language. It is Skeet. Its originator claims that it derives from an old Scandinavian word meaning "to shoot." Whether this derivation is correct, or otherwise, seems to be of academic interest. If Skeet derived only from arbitrary coinage it would still fill the bill nicely, for Skeet is a vivid, one-syllable word that suggests the flight of the target in the shotgun game it names. Of such words is language made.

Although scarcely a baker's dozen years old, Skeet in the United States alone has resulted thus far in the organization of about three thousand clubs with a total membership of at least sixty thousand shooters. Of the eighty-two million clay targets shot at during 1937 (most recent figures available), conservative estimate identifies no less than fifty million of these as being Skeet targets.

Of course you want to learn to shoot Skeet. I hope you want to learn the game for more than the smug reason that a rapidly growing number of "our best people" are taking to this exhilarating shotgun sport with enthusiasm. The ability to shoot Skeet decently well is more than a social attainment today. Indeed, it is more even than a tingling outdoor sport and a game of skill. There is a deeper psychological value to shooting Skeet that fits in very well with our scheme of living today. Under the tension of modern life we are apt to get to the point every once in a while where we toy with the idea of smashing something. Under the pressure of such periodic inward urge, probably common to all of us, it is far better to sally forth over the week-end and find emotional outlet in smashing Skeet targets. This is a more civilized procedure than smashing crockery in the cook's domain. In short, after a zestful afternoon spent in smashing Skeet targets with well-placed charges of chilled 9's out at the local Skeet club, or country club, you ought to be a better person to carry on—and to carry on with. You should be kinder to the children, less crotchety to your neighbors and business associates and a better all-round citizen.

However, there is usually an ant in every jam pot. By which I mean that if your destruction of Skeet targets falls short of your hopes on the score board, you will probably experience all the anguish and general lowness of spirit of the spanked child. How sharper than a serpent's tooth is a friend's kindly (?) inquiry as to your Skeet score when he knows confoundedly well (and you know he knows) that you handled your shotgun with the utter absence of grace of the scared dub, and that your scoring was wretched-er than wretched.

But take heart. Skeet is simple. Skeet is easy. As in every other outdoor sport, the trick of the business is to get started right. Then, having once got your teeth into the *principle* of the thing, never, never permit yourself to be deflected by well-meaning "expert" advisers who are usually eager to give you the low-down on how to hit 'em, with confusing variations warped to fit their own personal idiosyncracies.

Skeet is a versatile game. However, there is no assurance whatever that Skeet can transform you into a finished field shot. Only field shooting, actual experience in the uplands and on the marsh, can accomplish that triumph. But Skeet can carry you a longer step forward toward the skill of the finished field shot than any other regimented shotgun game.

Although they don't shoot quite the same kind of a Skeet game over in England that we do, the British frequently refer to Skeet as "a gun-game for the game-gun." Over here, in the land of its origin, Skeet is also referred to as "the off-season gun-game for the game shot." It seems to me I can cheerfully disagree with both of these descriptions of Skeet —for to me the implication is far too restricting. After all, Skeet is a game in its own right. Moreover, Skeet is constantly becoming more and more a game in its own right and entirely independent of its relationship to field shooting. I say this because upland game is becoming scarcer and scarcer in most parts of the United States, regardless of soothing reassurance on the part of sincere conservationists, politically administered state game departments and practical-minded groups who have a commercial interest in the existence of upland game. Such groups habitually vocalize eloquently in urging extermination of natural "predators." Seldom do they mention the deplorable fact that among the real predators, Man himself ranks foremost.

The truth of the matter is, as population rises and extends its boundaries, especially with quick motorized transportation, wild game recedes and dwindles in supply. The day is rapidly approaching, regrettably but inevitably, where public hunting rights will be so restricted and where natural game supply will be so depleted, that most of us who like to shoot will be forced to depend more or less on clay-target shooting for our gunning sport. Though of course those who care for that sort of thing will have increasing opportunity in the future to indulge (as far as their pocketbooks permit) in the "paid" type of shooting on artificially propagated birds, such as the ring-neck pheasant, the lumbering corn-fed "wild" duck, and so on.

Also, there are not a few persons who like to shoot, but who don't care to kill. This is a civilized attitude which commands respect, even though we may differ sharply in viewpoint.

But it does seem to me that Skeet, far from being a mere gun-game for the game-gun, or an off-season game for the upland gunner, is definitely slated to occupy an increasingly important place in its own right as an all-year outdoor game

[xi]

of skill for the man and woman who happen to like guns and shooting.

There is also another practical, though rather sinister side of Skeet. I refer to its potentialities as a training game for improving the accuracy of aerial rifle and machine gunnery in modern warfare. As a commander of a squadron of attack and pursuit 'planes in the warfare of the future, I should feel more confident of the safe return of my ships and men if the lads manning the machine guns were all good Skeet shots, already grooved in the mechanism of leading and timing on flying targets! Also, infantrymen armed with the latest type of semi-automatic service rifle should make it very hot indeed for low-flying ground-strafing 'planes—*if* these infantry troops have previously learned their "wingshooting" lessons in the peace-time sport of the Skeet field.

The vital angle in Skeet is that is includes the whole cycle of the wingshooting function—something that 16-yard gun-at-shoulder trapshooting does not accomplish. In Skeet the cycle of the shooting function starts with the gun in the down position, not at shoulder. Correct mounting of the gun has a terrifically important bearing on good wingshooting in the field. A graceful, sure-footed step forward is more certain when we start the step from the standing position with both feet on the ground. In the same way, more effective leverage, better timing, more rhythmic alignment on the flying target— all these result more naturally with starting the shooting cycle from the informal gun-down position of the Skeet field.

The mere reading, however, of this book on how to hit 'em at Skeet will scarcely result automatically in your becoming a crack Skeet shot. But the reading of this book *plus* careful (and plenteous) application of principles outlined herein should carry you well on the way towards shooting decently on the wing.

Probably the best of preliminary advice is to urge that you get rid of preconceived notions—particularly where the reader is a beginner, or at best a rather indifferent Skeet shot. In the matter of learning how to shoot Skeet you have, let us say, selected the author as your "doctor." This book, in a sense, represents a "prescription" you have paid for.

As you read through this book you will note a distinct departure from the usual familiar method of trying to tell the Skeet shooter exactly where to hold on each of the 24 shots (though 25 targets) in a round of Skeet. In the author's estimation, this method of trying to teach Skeet by telling the young shooter exactly where to hold on each shot is "dated" and always has been. Such instruction procedure must fall short of success, if only for the reason that it attempts to *reverse* the natural progression of cause-and-effect.

This book on how to hit 'em at Skeet proceeds in the *natural* sequence of cause-and-effect. This is a book of basic principles. Principles are considered first—for no two of us are exactly alike and no two of us can possibly function exactly alike in our shooting method. But all who shoot Skeet well *do* operate from a basis of fundamental principle.

In concluding this introduction of the subject, may I mention thanks to *Field & Stream* for the courtesy of permitting inclusion of certain photographic and other material used in this book—and also wish you luck?

THE GAME

SKEET has come a long way since a relative handful of us started shooting the game back in 1926. In that year, a small group of us living in the metropolitan suburban area of New York started the Valhalla Skeet Club —the third Skeet club organized in the United States. To show any interest at all in Skeet at that time meant that you were a field shot, a hunter. We came out to shoot Skeet dressed in hunting clothes. We used the same guns we carried in the field. At that time there was no such thing as the so-called Skeet gun. Curiously enough, though we didn't suspect it at the time, the game of Skeet was to considerably revise and improve the American field gun.

In the last few years, however, since Skeet has firmly established itself as a sport in its own right, in no wise dependent on the patronage of the field shot alone, the typical Skeet gun has emerged as a highly specialized smooth-bore instrument. For while we hold fast to the axiom that a field gun should be of medium, easy-carrying weight for tramping in the field, the special Skeet gun of today can be as weighty as a duck gun without in the least interfering with the shooter's skill. We are called upon to bear the weight of the heavier type of special Skeet gun only during the shooting function. Therefore, added gun-weight is no particular disadvantage. Indeed, to the shooter who might otherwise be sensitive to recoil, the heavy gun noticeably absorbs recoil that otherwise might result in bruised flesh and battered nerves.

Compared with the modern Skeet club, we were a motley crew back there in 1926. Our equipment was almost Spartan in its crude simplicity. Two flimsy traps threw the targets, one mounted on a rickety platform 10 feet above ground, the other slightly above ground level. The traps were entirely exposed, enclosed by no such structure as the modern trap house, and the trap loader was protected only by a sheet of corrugated iron nailed up in front of him. Incidentally, we took turns at functioning as "trap boys." Also, the trap loader was the puller. There was no central control even of the hand-operated type, let alone electrically operated with a timing device. Each club member who happened to be functioning as a "trap boy" at the moment, loaded and pulled at the shooter's command. One of the curious hand-downs from that day to this is that many Skeet shooters still call "Pull" for the hi-trap target and "Mark" for the lo-trap target. It was necessary, of course, to have two different calls back in 1926. This was the only way the "trap boys" could understand which target was meant to be thrown.

The Skeet field of that day and on up until ten years later, in the summer of 1936, was slightly different from the layout we use today. The trap houses, facing each other, were 40 yards apart, just the same as today. Station 8 was located midway between the two traps, also the same. Thus, stations 1, 7 and 8 have remained the same since the beginning of the game. Stations 2, 3, 4, 5 and 6 have been changed. Originally these stations were located equi-distant from each other on the arc of a semi-circle swung on a 20-yard radius from station 8. Today, these shooting stations have been moved inward, and the crossing-point of target flight has been moved outward. Today, the crossing-point of target flight has been moved out 6 yards beyond station 8. And the shooting stations from 2 to 6 are now located equi-distant from each other on an arc swung from the crossing-point of target flight on a 21-yard radius. Thus, instead of the targets being thrown

[2]

The 4-field lay-out of the Firestone Skeet Club, Akron, Ohio. The three center trap houses are of duplex type— hi-trap above and lo-trap below.

The gallery always follows the "hot" teams at the big shoots. Here is the Loantaka (N.J.) Skeet Team at a Lordship All-Bore Meet.

directly over the trap houses, on a line between station 1 and station 7, they are now thrown at an outward angle.

How and why the game was changed to "Angle" Skeet may be interesting to the reader. The idea was first brought to the author's attention by Mr. Field White of the Poly Choke Company in the summer of 1935. It was acknowledged that shooters were constantly exposed to a shower of shattered target fragments under the field lay-out of the old game, when shooting at stations 1, 7 and 8. A change in target line of flight to a pronounced outward angle would remove this hazard.

It was also suggested that with targets thrown at an outward angle, instead of on a straight line between the two trap houses, it would then be possible to locate a series of Skeet fields in a straight "down-the-line" lay-out. This would not only save space, but would also speed up the movement of shooters from one field to another in our larger state, regional and national matches. Owing to the fact that Skeet targets are shot in practically opposite directions, this matter of providing for sufficient space and safety area in laying out Skeet fields has always been a major problem—still is, as a matter of fact.

We were immediately struck by the significance of the proposed change and strongly suggested in the Skeet Department of *Field & Stream* that such a change be made in the standard Skeet lay-out. The idea was received with no great warmth at the moment, primarily because the Skeet game at that time was entirely under the control of a rival sporting magazine publisher.

Subsequent articles, however, stressing the safety features of the new proposed lay-out eventually got results. In the summer of 1936, at the Great Eastern Championships at Lordship, Conn., so-called "Angle" Skeet was initiated. In the National matches, following in September of that year, "Angle" Skeet became the official game. At that time we re-

[3]

ferred to the old game as "Shuttle" Skeet. However, both terms of distinction have now faded out and the official game today, with targets thrown at an outward angle, is simply Skeet.

The official Skeet field of today of course represents a compromise. When the line of target flight was changed to an outward angle, the shooting stations should have remained in their original positions—that is, located equidistant on a semi-circle swung from station 8 on the 20-yard radius. However, the sporting magazine publisher in control of Skeet didn't wish Skeet made more difficult for new shooters coming into the game. Perhaps he was quite right in this respect. Though I do feel that the original shooting stations would have made the new "Angle" game only slightly, if any, more difficult. Instead of a range of 21 yards, from station 4 to crossing-point of target flight, such as we have today, we would have at this point a shooting range of 26 yards. Surely, this is not excessive. In fact, it is well within the range of the No. 1 Skeet, or improved cylinder choke. A return to the original 20-yard-radius firing line may come along one of these days. I don't believe, though, that it would be a good idea to increase the range by further widening the outward angle of target flight. To widen this angle would make the station-8 shot easier—more of a short-range swinging shot, rather than the on-coming snap shot it is intended to be.

Of the twenty-four official rules and regulations of Skeet today, all might be boiled down under three general headings: (1) Safety, (2) Courtesy, (3) Sportsmanship. Insistence on 100-per-cent safe gun-handling is final and absolute. A man, or woman, who doesn't possess the poise, presence of mind and caution to be safe in his gun-handling has no business on a Skeet field. The shotgun at close range is the most terrible of all weapons. I have never seen a serious accident on the Skeet field, but they have happened—and I have seen

[4]

some close calls. But if you could ever see the result of a shotgun charge fired at close range (as I have seen in the field) the memory of it would be seared into your brain until the end of your days. Be careful!

Rule No. 1 of Skeet, with respect to loaded guns on the field, says: No loaded gun shall be allowed on the field except in the hands of the shooter *and when he is in position to shoot*. The italics are ours.

Rule No. 2, with regard to the number of shells in the gun, says: During the shooting of single targets, the shooter shall put but one shell in his gun at a time, with the exception that in registered shoots the management may permit the loading of two shells at any station, except station 8, providing said management assumes full responsibility for the exercising of this exception; but the management cannot compel the loading of two shells in the shooting of singles. More than two shells shall not be put in the gun at any time.

Our earnest advice to the beginner is to load but *one* shell in his gun at any time, except in the shooting of doubles.

As a beginner, if you adhere strictly to the rules of absolute safety in your gun-handling, you will be respected even though you miss every target in the string. But if you are *not* safe in your gun-handling, every person on the premises blessed with the sense God gave a goose will strive to give you the same avoidance with which he would treat a noisome odor. There is nothing so abhorrent to seasoned shooters as to see a beginner behave like a confused and embarrassed nitwit. Such a person's "popularity" is rated somewhat below that of a coiled rattlesnake.

On the score of Courtesy, breaches of etiquette are subtler and more easily forgivable—when committed by the beginner. Know in advance what not to do. Don't feel too embarrassed if you commit them. But don't keep on committing them repeatedly. The quality of forgiveness can be strained.

[5]

In this connection, here's a brief list of "don'ts" that you might paste in your hat-band: *Don't* keep your squad waiting in a last-minute rush for shells, or to finish a conversation with a friend on the side-lines. Get down to station 1 with the others in your squad as a group. *Don't* talk in a loud voice while any member of your squad is up at the station in shooting position. Some shooters who are sensitive to distraction resent audible talking and laughing while they are doing their best to break two targets.

Stand directly back of the shooter and not too close to him. Some shooters keenly sense the close proximity of gunners standing behind them and resent this, though they may say nothing about it. *Don't* ever, under any circumstances, practice swinging and aiming on a squad mate's target while he is shooting. You know your gun is unloaded, sure. But no one else can be sure. Besides, the rules of Skeet say that your gun must be open and empty—until you step up to shoot in your turn. When it is your turn to shoot, step up to the station with gun open and empty. Then, and only at that moment, shall you load your gun—with a single cartridge if you happen to be shooting singles—with two cartridges if you happen to be shooting a double.

Your gun is now loaded and closed and you have two charges of sudden death under your trigger finger—so keep that muzzle outwardly pointed. If anyone should be rude enough to ask you a question at this moment, or otherwise engage you in conversation, calmly break your gun and delay your shooting (to remind him of the discourtesy!) answering him over your shoulder without turning around. Never, never turn around with a loaded gun in your hands. If there is any delay in offering you your target, through trap break-down or other cause, open your gun and unload before stepping away from the firing station.

After you have fired your two shots, break your gun and turn immediately away from the station—and turn to the right. The next man up is coming in on your left side. It is annoying for a shooter stepping up to be awkwardly run headlong into by a confused shooter leaving the firing station. Also, leave the firing station smartly. It is annoying to the whole squad to have a dumb gunner fire both shots and then stand stupidly staring into space, wondering why, where, or how he missed. Whether you hit or miss, get away from the station quickly. Nobody else in the squad is interested in your problems, nor in your post-mortems. Skeedaddle!

In addition to Safety and Courtesy, also observe the rules of Sportsmanship. The latter has entirely to do with gun-position and in quick and silent acceptance of the referee's decision. There are chisellers in Skeet, just as in every other game. They are an odious breed. Chisellers on Skeet's rule No. 3, regarding correct gun-position, occasionally, I believe, come by the habit more or less innocently. Guard against this. Skeet's rule on gun-position is as clear-cut and definite as it can be expressed. Obey it in spirit as well as in technicality. The rule says that your gun-butt shall be far enough below your shoulder so that some portion of it is visible beneath your arm. There are within-the-law methods of beating the game here, unfortunately. Some shooters lean far forward, so that the outstretched arm is bound to raise the level of the gun-stock and bring it nearer the shoulder. Others raise the elbow, as the off-hand rifle shot does, and thus get by on the technicality of "visible" stock below the elbow. Such shooters afford a humorous spectacle, in a way. Like the ostrich, who is supposed (erroneously) to stick his head in the sand to hide, these shooters are kidding only themselves. Their chiselling is glaringly apparent; but there is little the average referee can (or will) do about it.

If you start right, you will be less likely to drift into this sort of chiselling. I am confident it can be drifted into unconsciously by the over-eager shooter who in every other respect is normally honest. But such a shooter isn't a pretty spectacle by any stretch of the imagination. Also, entirely irrespective of whether his chiselling is of the unconscious and over-eager variety, he is cataloged as a "sharper" by all the lads and lasses in the game who know their way around.

2

FIELD LAY-OUT

~~~~~~

SKEET enthusiasts frequently write to me, asking advice on how properly to lay out the modern Skeet field. They want to know how much area is required for safety; how the field should be faced for best sunlight conditions; and in general how they may go about setting up a Skeet shooting field that will be as nearly perfect as practicable.

First of all, let's face the field in the proper direction. By "facing" the field I mean the establishment of the direction of the imaginary line running from station 4 out through station 8 and thence through the crossing-point of target flight.

In the northern hemisphere, generally speaking, this line from station 4 out through station 8 should point to the northeast; and in the southern hemisphere, to the southeast. The reason is obvious.

With the field so laid out (taking the northern hemisphere, for example) the shooter standing at station 1 will shoot at his outgoing target in a southeasterly direction. The only time of the day that sunlight conditions might be a little objectionable from this position would be in the early forenoon; and of course the lower altitude of the winter sun makes shooting from station 1 on such a field a little more difficult. However, most Skeet shooting is done from late forenoon to late afternoon and evening. Sun glare can't be entirely eliminated, regardless of which direction you face

[9]

your field, and the northeasterly facing offers best average lighting conditions. You can't get away from sun glare entirely, due to the wide variation in direction of shots fired on the Skeet field. Anyway, that's what anti-glare sun glasses are made for.

Specifications for the building of both hi- and lo-trap houses are pretty well standardized today. Valuable assistance in this direction may be secured from the Skeet Departments of Remington Arms Company, Bridgeport, Conn., Western Cartridge Company, East Alton, Ill. and also from the National Skeet Shooting Association, 275 Newbury Street, Boston, Mass.

The two trap houses should be located 40 yards apart, with their trap openings facing each other. Station 8 is located midway between, 20 yards from each trap house. The hi-trap is on the left, the lo-trap on the right side of the field. Station 1 is located immediately in front of the facing of the hi-trap house, while station 7 is located immediately in front of the lo-trap house. Thus, the 40-yard base line of the Skeet field, from station 1 through station 8 to station 7, is established.

Perpendicular to this base line, the crossing-point of target flight is located 6 yards out from station 8; and with this crossing-point of target flight fixed, the other shooting stations 2, 3, 4, 5 and 6 are located equi-distant on an arc swung from the crossing-point of target flight on a 21-yard radius.

Whoever your builder is, insist that he provide and place in secure position at the trap openings the heavy sheet-metal guards that shield the trap boy within the house from flying shot pellets. Failure to provide such officially adopted safety feature might easily result in damage suits arising from injuries to trap boys.

On the average Skeet field, even today, the odd and old-fashioned habit persists of putting in upright posts at each shooting station. These are not necessary. Posts like this not

only spoil the looks of a Skeet field, but frequently act as annoying mental hazards to shooters. Moreover, such a post frequently prevents a shooter from functioning according to
the rules of Skeet as formulated by the National Skeet Shooting Association. This rule states that the shooter shall stand
within a 30-inch circle. But if a post is sticking up at the

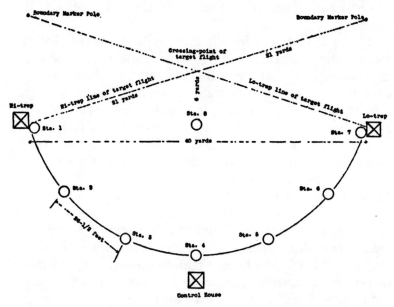

station, how can you expect a shooter to stand in the area
represented by a 15-inch radius—unless he straddles the
post!

The beautiful 4-field Skeet lay-out of the Massachusetts
Fish & Game Association, on its 3000-acre game preserve
near Boston, was the first (as far as we know) to eliminate the
useless eye-sores as represented by posts or stakes embedded
in the ground at each station. The shooting stations on these
four fine fields are marked by 6-inch sections of iron cylinder
embedded in the ground and filled with beach sand. This
circular metal "rim" is 30 inches in diameter, or thereabouts..

[11]

The exact diameter is not particularly important, unless too far exceeded. The shooter naturally stands in the center anyway, and the sand affords even, secure and clean footing. I strongly recommend that clubs throughout the country adopt this better plan and do away entirely with the unkempt spectacle of having posts, or stakes, in varying stages of decay and dilapidation, stuck around the firing-line of the field.

The control house for the trap puller is usually located immediately behind station 4. This house should be built high enough so that the puller, seated, can always see out over the heads of the shooters, to keep score on dead and lost targets. Equipment for either manual or electric control, as well as the two traps, may be secured either of Remington or Western make. Both concerns furnish complete equipment, from traps to electrical timers, which latter according to the rules of Skeet should be regulated to allow a delay between the shooter's call for the target and its appearance of a variable interval from instantaneous to approximately three seconds' delay. Both concerns also supply targets, the well-known Blue Rock target being manufactured by Remington and the White Flyer target by Western. Other brands of targets are available, made by Black Products Company, Mineral Springs Lime Company and others.

Properly built trap houses on the Skeet field are of substantial construction. Particularly in the support of the trap unit, sufficiently heavy timbers should be used to insure absolutely solid support. Lack of strong support will result in trap vibration—which not only is wearing on the trap, but which will result in costly target waste.

On a regulation Skeet field, the target from the hi-trap house should begin its flight 10 feet above ground level. Flight from the lo-trap house should begin at a point 3 feet above ground level. Both traps should be so adjusted as to give a target trajectory 15 feet above ground level at the crossing-point of the two lines of target flight. Spring tension in the throwing arm of the trap should be so adjusted as to throw the target a total distance of from 55 to 60 yards under still-air conditions.

Skeet shooters frequently write to me, inquiring as to the velocity of the Skeet target—not only the target's initial velocity, but its remaining velocity at the time it is shot at by the average shooter from the different firing-stations on the Skeet field. This information is available through tests conducted by Mr. Wallace H. Coxe, ballistic engineer of the DuPont Company, some years back, and reported in his interesting treatise *Smokeless Shotgun Powders*. The tests were made with an oscillograph in a manner similar to that employed for determining the velocity of shot charges, using screens placed along the trajectory of the clay target. The regulation trapshooting target is thrown an extreme range of 50 yards. The Skeet target is a slightly faster target, with extreme range of between 55 and 60 yards. The Skeet target, Mr. Coxe found, leaves the trap at an initial average velocity of 96 ft. per second. At the 20-yard point in its trajectory its remaining velocity is 52 ft. per second. At 25 yards, remaining velocity is 47 ft. per second. At 30 yards, remaining velocity is 43 ft. per second. At 50 yards (8 yards out of bounds) the target has slowed down to 35 ft. per second.

In terms of elapsed time interval, the target requires .9 second to travel 20 yards, 1.2 seconds to travel 25 yards, 1.5 seconds to travel 30 yards, and 3.1 seconds to travel 50 yards.

Interpolating from these laboratory test figures, we believe it a fair approximation to state that on the station-8 targets the average gunner sees his target, mounts his gun and fires within a space of about ⅜ of a second. An appallingly short interval of time in which to mount, point a gun and fire, you say? Not at all difficult—as you will discover for yourself later on. A second is a longer space of time than most of us realize. I know a few shooters who can mount their guns and smash the station-8 targets in ½ second, or less. Mr. Ed McGivern, the famous revolver shot can fire five shots double-action from the cylinder-gun (and hit with them) in less than ⅖ of a second.

By no means the least difficulty to be encountered in the selection of a suitable site for a Skeet field is to insure a safe "danger zone." Shotgun pellets from smallest size up to No. 7½'s are harmless after they travel 250 yards. However, I've seldom visited a Skeet club where at least some of the members, at some time during the non-game-shooting season, didn't use the remnants of their autumn supply of game-shooting cartridges. Game cartridges are frequently loaded with shot pellets of larger size than the regulation Skeet No. 9's. When shot sizes go up to 5's, 4's and even 2's, then you will understand why the National Skeet Shooting Association leaned backward in its extra generous extension of the boundaries of the danger zone.

The N.S.S.A. recommends that a danger zone be provided of such area as to be included in a radius of 300 yards from each trap house. Even if one could be certain that shot sizes would never be used of larger size than the 9's which are standard in Skeet shooting, then I'd still say the 300-yard boundaries of the danger zone would be not at all excessive. For there is always the danger of the so-called "balled" shot load—shot pellets fused together and leaving the gun muzzle as a more or less solid "projectile." Moreover, small shot, like 9's, are the sizes most subject to "balling."

Unless the Skeet field is so ideally situated that it can face northeast over a swampy tract, where human beings will scarcely ever venture, a good idea also is to have the entire danger zone within good visibility, so that incautious individuals, or those who are unwarned of the hazard, may be clearly seen before they come within dangerous range of the guns.

The foregoing is an important detail to watch out for in

advance. An injunction that would stop shooting and completely disrupt the pleasant week-end recreation of a whole Skeet club, might easily result from even the slightest non-serious injury to the members or friends of families of adjacent land-owners who might (unseen) stray too far within the boundaries of the danger zone in their walks through the fields and woods.

There is one feature of the modern Skeet field that I'd like to go on record as being strongly against—this is the board-walk firing-line. In the first place, there is nothing like the confidence one gains from feeling his two feet planted securely on good old terra firma. Second, any idea of installing a board-walk should be discarded on the basis of its threat to 100-per-cent safety. Wet boards are slippery. Wet boards covered over with a thin film of snow are treacherous. Also, boards that are close to the ground decay quickly—and I have seen broken boards trip a shooter and otherwise seriously annoy a whole squad—if only for the reason that every sensible man in the squad realizes the potentialities of a gunner falling with a loaded gun in his hands!

There is one more point in Skeet field construction that it may be useful to note. This is in connection with putting up the protective safety fence between fields, where two or more Skeet fields are laid down-the-line at a big club. When these protective fences were first built, they were simply made in the form of flat board fences. The reverberating sound between two such board fences was most annoying. There would be a series of reports as the sound bounced back and forth between the two protective fences. However, some smart acoustics engineer solved this problem a year or so ago by making this protective fence of "baffle" type. That is, the boards are nailed on both sides of the 2 x 4 frame— and the boards are staggered in their placement, the board on one side covering the space left open on the other side.

[15]

3

APPAREL

~~~~~~

A HIGHER percentage of men buy and wear ready-made clothes today, because the manufacturers of such clothing pay strict attention to the matter of fabric quality, styling and tailoring. No such general catering to the demands of the buyer is readily apparent, however, among the manufacturers of shooting clothes. The average shooting coat, for example, is still made to fit its wearer like a potato sack—and the stiff unfriendly material it is usually made of doesn't seem vastly superior to the stuff the potato sack is made of, either. In short, the average ready-made shooting coat of today is practically the same identical model offered back around the turn of the century, when the late Colonel Theodore Roosevelt and his Rough Riders made the country khaki-conscious.

How a hunter wearing one of these stiff and unyielding canvas misfits can be expected to be at his best in the delicate art of wingshooting, particularly under the conditions enforced by the flush and flight of game in our American style of rough shooting—this is something I can't answer. I do suspect though, that the real answer is that the gunner just doesn't do his best work.

The whole trouble with the average medium-price hunting coat is that its manufacturer tries to make it fulfill too many requirements. Of course, the manufacturers' answer to this would be that the coat is made to meet the demands of the shooter. Might be something in this, too. If so, I think perhaps we shooting writers are at fault for not properly educating the shooting public—and maybe it is high time we accomplished something in this direction.

The manufacturer of the average ready-made hunting coat includes so many "virtues" that no wonder it is usually lacking in that highest and most vital requirement—in the respect that it simply doesn't fit the shooter comfortably. It is made briar-proof, water-proof, chill-proof—and to cap the complex absurdity, is invariably provided with excessive game-carrying capacity, not to mention excess pocket room for more ammunition than any sensible modern gunner would ever think of carting around on his person.

A proper shooting jacket should be made of light, closely-woven material, just heavy enough to provide the shooter with a slight extra margin of protection against chill, wind, rain, or snow. Your modern gunner isn't very far from his car anyhow. If he gets thoroughly wet he comes back to the car for a change of jacket, or an entire change of clothing. The modern method of hunting, under motorized transportation, is to spot-hunt selected cover areas. We no longer leg it for a whole day before returning to the horse-and-buggy for the homeward trip.

Also, the smart hunter doesn't go burrowing through briars and blackberry thorns in quest of his game, much after the fashion of the fabulous gentleman in the nursery rhyme who jumped into the bramble bush. The smart gunner stands out in the open where he has all the better of the bargain on the flush of game, depending on his dog to work the brambled cover; or else chunking in a rock or a stick to start any game that may be lying within. For protection against rain, he may even carry a light slicker, folded into a package not much larger than a tobacco pouch. And as for ammunition-toting, a half-dozen shells in his pocket and two in his gun will—I'm sorry to say—see him safely through any bit of selected cover in these hapless days of scarce and hard-to-find game.

[17]

As far as correct design in the Skeet jacket is concerned, only a few of our custom tailors have thus far made any real progress toward giving the shooter what he really needs. Practically all of the ready-made jackets of some years back were equipped with leather shoulder pads. Such a shoulder pad is frequently a nuisance to the Skeet shooter. It is quite all right for the trapshooter, who mounts his gun before calling for the target. But too often my own gun-butt has caught on such a leather shoulder pad—which not only may result in a clean miss on that particular shot, but also makes the gunner apprehensive over the possibility of similar interference on every shot he fires thereafter. Such a jacket may even get the shooter into the habit of pushing his gun-butt out from his body—so that he brings it up and returns it in to his shoulder—which not only makes unnecessary movement and induces mental distraction, but also happens to be the wrong way for the gunner to mount his gun.

The Skeet jacket should not be made of slippery material, such as wool. The average gun-butt is rather slippery on wool unless a rubber recoil pad is attached, in which case the raw rubber will surely catch occasionally and perhaps momentarily hang up the shooter's gun.

One of the most excellent Skeet-jacket materials the author has found is Safari cloth, trademarked and supplied by Abercrombie & Fitch of New York. However, the Skeet jackets ready-made of this material and sold by A. & F. are usually exceedingly poor in fit, unless one happens to strike a good fit by luck. But if the Skeet jacket can be custom-tailored for the shooter, made of Safari cloth, and made up without any shoulder piece of leather or other material—such a tailored jacket should represent about the last word in correct design and material—if the tailor knows his business.

As regards carrying one's ammunition about the Skeet field, I definitely prefer to carry the shells in my jacket pock-

The Skeet field is a focal point of interest at Hot Springs, Va.

Hundreds of Skeet fields dot the country today—week-end recreation spots for thousands of scatter-gun enthusiasts.

ets, with pockets positioned well toward the front of the body. I prefer this arrangement to the belted shell-pouch made to fit a single box of ammunition. I prefer to carry the shells in my pocket because their weight keeps the sides, and particularly the front, of my jacket smooth so that no wrinkles are sticking out to catch the gun-butt in the mounting—and even in the best designed belted Skeet jacket such wrinkles are bound to stick out, here and there, because of the motions of the arms and body.

Moreover, I always like to carry the greater weight of ammunition on the right-hand side (in the case of the right-handed gunner) because of the leverage advantage. Thus, the left arm is practically unhampered (or hampered only at a minimum) in slightly raising the weight of shells in the left-hand pocket. My system is to load as many cartridges into the right-hand pocket as it will hold, then put the remainder on the left side—and in shooting, to begin using cartridges from the left-hand pocket. Might be well for you to copy this procedure—and of course reverse it in case you shoot from the left side.

In the matter of headgear, I feel that the visored cap is superior in every respect to the brimmed hat. The visor of the cap helps protect the eyes from excessive light glare, yet permits unobstructed vision out at the sides. The brimmed hat, particularly if the brim is overly wide, sometimes flaps down under windy shooting conditions, almost enough to obscure vision. It is most disconcerting in a small but subtle way to have this happen, Therefore, my choice for spring, winter and autumn shooting on the Skeet field is the cap—and in summer shooting, the ordinary eye-shade, or some variation of it, works admirably—so long as one's unprotected head isn't exposed for too long to the direct rays of hot summer sunlight.

In the matter of footgear, beware of the slippery soles of ordinary street or business shoes, particularly if shooting from sodded firing stations. Slippery leather soles give one a baffling, apprehensive sense of insecurity. This matter of having the feet in secure, gripping contact with the ground is vitally important—don't overlook it! Ordinary sneakers or tennis shoes are good for summer wear. Hobnailed golf shoes are excellent. But avoid wearing shoes soled with crepe rubber—for this material, when new, not only gives the shooter a too-springy and wobbly contact with the ground, but on wet clay or wet boards is extremely slippery and treacherous —wickedly dangerous if the shooter should slip and fall with loaded gun, though I have never seen this happen—nor do I wish to, ever.

In the matter of dressing for winter shooting, don't dress too heavily. As a matter of fact, most of us dress too heavily in winter anyhow. We would be healthier if we wore less and exercised more while out in the air. The average Skeet field usually has a warm club house nearby—or in the case of the country club, temporary or fixed accommodations are fairly close at hand where the shooter may take refuge between rounds.

Excessive clothing not only restricts freedom of movement, so necessary in good gun-handling, but may also actually change the familiar fit of your pet Skeet gun. A ½-inch padding of extra clothing on your shoulder means ½-inch added to the length of your gunstock—and any change as considerable as half an inch at this point may throw you off badly in your scoring.

4

THE GUN

~~~~~~

JUST as the top-notchers in golf more or less set the style for the rank and file of players in the matter of selection and design of clubs, so it is probably true that the match headliners in Skeet more or less set the fashion in Skeet guns. You may argue that a cross-section of a distinct minority is not necessarily representative of the majority—and on general principles you would probably be correct. After all, only about 5 per cent of the Skeet shooters in the United States shoot in registered competition. But just the same, I am reasonably certain that from the way the Skeet game is going today—all in the direction of a distinct and separate shooting game in its own right, and without its former close association with field shooting—that an analysis of the types of guns used by registered match Skeet shooters will reveal average preference with fair accuracy.

Accordingly, it will be interesting for the reader to know what types of guns are in most popular use in the big registered matches, such as the Great Eastern Championships at Lordship, Connecticut, and also in the National Championship matches—the two outstanding annual competitive Skeet events in the country. Here's the way preference is divided among competitive shooters attending these big matches:

Of the 215 shooters competing in the All-Bore match at the Great Eastern Championships at Lordship last summer (1938) 46 per cent shot autoloaders; 34.4 per cent shot pump guns; 14 per cent shot over-and-unders; and only 5.6 per cent shot the conventional side-by-side double gun.

Following soon after, in September, at the National Championship matches held in Tulsa, Oklahoma, of the 237 shooters who competed in the All-Bore event, 67.1 per cent shot autoloaders; 18.1 per cent shot pump guns; 4.2 per cent shot over-and-unders; and 10.6 per cent shot side-by-side double guns.

It would be optimistic to say that there is any observable parallel as to gun preference in comparing these two shoots. The reason is obvious. By far the greater number of shooters competing at Lordship came from the Eastern seaboard. While out at the 1938 National Championship matches, relatively few eastern shooters were present, most of the entry list coming from the middle of the country and farther west. In fact, five states—Oklahoma, Kansas, California, Texas and Missouri furnished no less than 50 per cent of the entries.

A somewhat more reliable guide as to Skeet-gun preference throughout the country is revealed when we combine both groups and break down gun preference on a percentage basis, thus:

Of the 452 shooters competing in the All-Bore events at Lordship and the National Championships in 1938—57.1 per cent shot autoloaders; 25.9 per cent shot pump guns; 8.8 per cent shot over-and-unders; and 8.2 per cent shot side-by-side double guns.

This makes out a pretty strong case for the autoloader, without further argument. The figures speak for themselves. Optimism with reference to the continued popularity of the autoloader in Skeet is also reflected in the fact that Winchester will shortly (by the time this book appears in print, I understand) place on the market a new autoloading shotgun.

Strictly from the game shooter's point of view, and particularly from the standpoint of the conservationist, it would seem fool-hardy on the part of Winchester to bring out a new autoloading shotgun at a time when this type of gun may quite possibly be further legislated against as far as its use in game shooting is concerned. It is forbidden to use the autoloading shotgun in game shooting throughout Canada. The autoloader is similarly forbidden, or at least has its multiple-shot feature seriously curtailed, in several states on this side of the Canadian boundary. Why then do you suppose a concern like Winchester, with a fair reputation for commercial sagacity, is about to place a new autoloading shotgun on the market?

The answer, it seems to me, is that Winchester shrewdly foresees that Skeet is rapidly becoming more and more a game in its own right—and possibly becoming more and more widely separated from its earlier association with upland shooting. Skeet is definitely a game that smart people in the better income brackets are taking to enthusiastically today. A hundred or more golf and country clubs throughout the nation have turned to Skeet as a winter sport. People want to be able to shoot Skeet decently well today for the same reason they want to be able to ride a horse decently well; simply because one should be able to do both. Intercollegiate Skeet matches are coming into vogue—Yale against Princeton, Princeton against West Point—and this is just the beginning. Skeet has started on the second interval of its ascendancy. And this is why Winchester, already successful in having sold a generous share of the modern double-gun market with its excellent Model 21, is following the lead of Skeet shooters' choice and turning its productive genius to the manufacture of a new autoloading Skeet gun.

There is just one thought in connection with buying a Skeet gun that it might be valuable for the beginner to bear in mind. I refer to the variety of shotgun gauges commonly used on the Skeet field today. It has long been my belief that the only gun a Skeet shooter should use is that particular type, gauge and weight of gun with which he can break the greatest number of Skeet targets out of a hundred. In other words, shoot with the weight and gauge of gun that you can do your best shooting with. Don't bother with other guns, however much the fad beckons. It's a wise gunner who uses but one gun. Also, it's a phenomenal gunner who is capable of knowing *well* more than one gun.

There is scarcely a seasoned veteran on the big-time Skeet circuit today who does not possess a rack of Skeet guns, ranging in gauge all the way from .410 to 12. Why should this state of affairs exist? Surely not because the shooter in question has his shooting in the least benefited by changing from one gun to the other. Yet I have heard it said many a time, by those who should know better, and you no doubt will hear it said many a time also—that "the .410 is the best trainer for 12-gauge match shooting a man can possibly use."

This is an interesting idea—an idea which on the surface seems to have much to it. Unfortunately, it has no basis of fact. Regardless of the point that the ability to place a small shot load accurately would seem to argue for greatly-increased scoring ability when going to the 12-gauge shot load—there is the little (but mighty) matter of totally different recoil, weight and handling qualities in the two guns, the .410 as compared with the 12-gauge.

The average .410 gun has an entirely different weight and balance than the average 12-gauge gun. Second, with smaller shot charge and narrower shot pattern, the .410 shooter must needs hold more closely, be even meticulous and painstaking in his aiming. And those of us who have made a close analytical study of the art of shotgun shooting over a sufficient number of years to know what we are about, have a very apt descriptive term for the shooter who becomes "meticulous" or "painstaking" in his shotgun shooting. We call him a "putterer."

Puttering, I might add, is a vice—has no place in the real

art of wingshooting, opponents to the contrary notwithstanding. The whole technique of the .410 gun is different. Yet our Skeet-shooting friend who believes it his solemn duty to engage in the whole gamut of Skeet's matches, from .410 sub-small-bore up to 12-gauge, labors under the unfortunate idea that he is doing the best possible thing to groom his skill for the important all-bore matches by drilling himself with the .410-gauge with its ½-ounce shot charge.

I have seen too many shooters go through the preliminary .410-gauge and 28-gauge matches—and good shooters, too, who might have gotten somewhere—or at least who had the potentiality for getting somewhere in the big match—yet by the time they arrived up at the "all-bore" 12-gauge event, they had apparently lost the feel of the 12-gauge gun.

Why do we have our major Skeet matches cluttered up with these small-gauge preliminary matches? In this connection, perhaps it is high time someone let the pussy-cat out of the sack. Supposing for the moment that you are one of those trusting innocents who doesn't realize what's going on about him—which of course you are not—what, do you suppose, is the real reason why we have in practically every major tournament the .410-gauge sub-small-bore match, the small-bore or 28-gauge match, the 20-gauge match, all in addition and leading up to the *piéce de resistance* represented by the all-bore or 12-gauge match? Well, primarily this sweet little arrangement was inaugurated merely to put more sugar and cream into somebody's coffer—and of course this is all entirely square and on the up and up, you understand. After all, Skeet was originated by a sporting magazine—and though the worthy originators had the devil's own time selling the shooting industry on the Skeet idea, it remained later the duty and pleasure of the sporting magazine in question to serve its masters.

Anyway, there have been a lot of .410-gauge and 28-gauge guns sold and, what's more, the sellers and the buyers seem to have had a good time selling and buying; so no particular harm has been done. But let's call a spade a spade and not retreat behind any high-falutin idea of the importance of small-bore skeet shooting. If you think it is important, I only ask you to watch the reaction of the gallery at any of the small-bore matches. The "gallery" is practically non-existent. And it isn't until the boys begin stirring around, in moving up to the firing line for the big-bore match, that the customers really begin to bestir themselves and get a little bit excited. And in the meantime, slogging around through the small-bore matches, may be a dozen or more good gun-swingers who are wearing themselves down and disrupting their 12-gauge timing merely for the sake of a piddling .410-gauge or 28-gauge title.

There is absolutely no intent in the foregoing to influence any newcomer to Skeet against indulging in the pleasures of shooting the lighter-than-12-gauge gun. In fact, I think that Skeet is almost ideally suited, as a game, to the 20-gauge gun with its standard ⅞-ounce shot charge. Also, we might as well admit right here that the only logical reason which makes a man go to lighter gauge, lighter gun-weight and lighter shot load, with attendant lighter recoil, is that the benefits conferred by the smaller gauge actually improve his shooting. In short, we ought to change to a smaller gun only if the smaller gun enables us to kill a larger percentage of our targets. Maybe we can swing the lighter gauge more easily. Maybe we stand the recoil of the lighter gauge better. Anyway, there are those of us who shoot better with the lighter gauge and we should stick to it.

However, we Americans are born and bred to the adage that "nothing succeeds like success." We aspire to perfection in all things, and this applies to home runs in baseball, just as it does to holes-in-one in golf and 100-straights on the Skeet field. So the thread of my advice, with little variation, is this: Select and use exclusively (1) the type and gauge of gun with which you can break your highest scores at Skeet; or (2) the gun you get the most fun out of shooting.

In selecting a Skeet gun for yourself, let's take a look at all four types, in the order of their popularity among registered match Skeet shooters of the country:

THE AUTOLOADER

Take the autoloader first, favored on the basis of figures already quoted by more than half of those who shoot Skeet for all there is in it.

Three autoloaders are on the market at present—Remington, Browning and Savage. The first two named, in my opinion, are on a par. All three are made on the John Browning design, patents on which have expired. I have always considered the Browning a little the best-made and best-finished autoloader on the market, its parts being made in Belgium. However, the Remington Sportsman makes up the slight inequality in workmanship by being slightly the better balanced gun of the two. So, in my feeling, the Browning and Remington are practically on a par. Savage has done a very smart thing in equipping its 3-shot Skeet model autoloader with the Cutts Compensator as standard factory equipment. The Compensator is immensely popular with all shooters and deservedly so, though we shall reserve comment on this muzzle attachment until later.

While the Browning and Savage autoloaders are available only in 12- and 16-gauge, the Remington Sportsman comes in 12-, 16- and 20-gauge.

Gun-weight apparently means little to the Skeet shooter. I have seen little boys in knee-pants, as well as women of slight build, swing 8-pound autoloaders on the Skeet field with excellent scoring results. In Skeet, unlike field gunning, the shooter is not called upon to bear the weight of his gun except in the shooting function. Therefore, weight (so long as it is not actually beyond the strength of the shooter to handle it in the shooting function) may be, and quite probably is, a definite advantage in supplying the extra inertia which absorbs and softens recoil effect.

However, the amount of gun-weight one can handle in Skeet shooting is more or less dependent, I believe, on one's temperament as well as actual physical strength. For my own part, I have always disliked the weighty heavy-handling gun, though forced to admit that even excessive weight does lend smoothness and steadiness to one's swing—once the piece is in motion. The heavy gun is particularly desirable in most wildfowl shooting, particularly in pass shooting, in which latter type of sport the heavy gun does much to soften the pounding of heavy loads fired at high angle. But to me, personally, the slow and momentarily unyielding inertia of the heavy gun definitely detracts from the subtlety and delicacy which, to some of us, seem more or less inseparable from the art of wingshooting. For this reason I prefer, and shoot at Skeet, a 12-gauge side-by-side double gun weighing about 6¾ pounds.

A personal factor that might be mentioned here is that I am apparently less sensitive to recoil—or perhaps more adept at "rolling with the punch" than the average gunner—so that the 6¾-pound gun with the standard American 12-gauge Skeet load of 3 drams equivalent powder charge and 1⅛-ounce of No. 9 shot is not at all discomforting. However, we should probably leave personal preference out of this; for my background is that of the field shot, therefore not to be considered in view of the fact that average Skeet gun preference has already been expressed by overwhelming percentage ratio.

The cold hard arithmetic of the score-board is all in favor of the 12-gauge gun, of cylinder boring, and quite regardless of the weight of the gun itself. But there are two extremes of shooters, I believe, who are frequently better suited by (1) a light gun with lighter shot charge, or (2) with a gun of lighter weight yet handling the same standard 12-gauge shot load.

At the one extreme is the beginner, who, generally speaking, will do better to start off at the initial stage of his Skeet shooting with a gun of such weight as renders it easily within his control. Also, the recoil of his gun should be easily within the acceptance of his untrained muscles and nerves. To satisfy this rational fundamental, I sincerely believe the beginner at Skeet would do better, for six months and possibly longer, to do his shooting with a 6 to 6½-pound 20-gauge double gun with both barrels choked not closer than improved cylinder. And I would also recommend barrels not longer than 26 inches.

At the other extreme of those shooters who generally do better shooting with less gun-weight, I would class the seasoned performer on game birds in the field, who has discovered through years of shooting that medium gun-weight offers maximum speed and ease of responsiveness with minimum muscular effort. Such a shooter need not be considered here, for he is a skilled performer in the field and needs no coaching. Also, his yardstick of measurement, as far as his personal enjoyment is concerned, is simply that degree of proficiency he can ultimately attain with his favorite equipment. In short, he would rather perform creditably with his medium-weight 12-gauge game gun than to enter into the competitive grind against match shots with a heavy-weight, Compensator-equipped 12-gauge autoloader. Anyway, it is doubtful whether he would add more than two or three targets in a hundred to his score, at most—simply because he hasn't in his make-up what we might call the "competitive stamina."

So, aside from these two extremes, which seem better

adapted to medium gun-weight, I'd say unhesitatingly that the 7½ to 8½-pound gun comes nearest to meeting average requirements on the Skeet field.

SINGLE ALIGNMENT

Single alignment is another important feature that dictates the choice of gun to be used exclusively at Skeet. The single-alignment gun has always been top choice with the clay-target shooter. Single alignment is a feature of such Skeet guns as the autoloader, the pump gun and the over-and-under. Single alignment—that is, the existence of only a single barrel to aim over—offers an advantage clearly recognized wherever clay targets are shot at, whether at the 16-yard trap or on the Skeet field.

The general feeling is that single alignment offers opportunity for nicer precision in aiming. The twin muzzles of the conventional side-by-side double gun, most top-flight trap and Skeet shooters feel, cover too much area in the region of the flying target. Also, there's a tendency on the part of certain shooters to aim over either the right or the left tube of the side-by-side double gun, instead of over the center rib, thus resulting in the error called "cross-firing."

On the other hand, there are those staunch supporters of the side-by-side double gun who declare that the broad sighting plane of the side-by-side double gun is an actual advantage in accurate wingshooting—since this broad, easily-visible sighting plane is readily kept in view by the power of the sub-conscious eye, thereby releasing conscious vision for closer observance of the target's speed and direction of flight.

Both viewpoints are solidly founded on fact, so take your choice. The side-by-side double gun, however, can be straighter-stocked, so that the shooter can't get his eye too far down behind the breech and thus have too much of the horizontal plane obliterated in the immediate area of the target. Or maybe it all boils down to which type of shooter you will eventually turn out to be—as to whether you will prefer the single alignment of the autoloader, pump gun, or over-and-under—or whether you will turn to the side-by-side double gun as the weapon of your choice. You will make either one or the other your choice on the basis of performance. Don't be influenced by anyone's prejudice, either for or against, and least of all your own private prejudices. Use the gun—and stick to it—with which you find you can do your best shooting.

After quite a few years of observing hundreds and hundreds of gunners, both in the game field, also at 16-yard trapshooting and on the Skeet field, I have come to the conclusion that gunners, generally speaking, may be classified in two groups. First, there are the *aimers*. Second, there are the *approximators*. Among the aimers, you find a good many outand-out trapshooters. Among the approximators, you find a generous sprinkling of game shots.

Now of course, these two groups are in no sense to be considered "east and west and never the twain shall meet"— because, in my estimation, the really finished shotgun performer is *both* and resorts to either style of shooting, according to the demands enforced by target flight.

These two distinct groups of shooters invariably misunderstand each other. Each has little use for the other's style. Your precision aimer, most frequently met with in 16-yard trapshooting (and just about as frequently encountered in the big-time Skeet matches) may rather contemptuously refer to the approximator as merely a snap shot. And the approximator, getting even on his score, will refer to the aimer as a pokey, slow performer.

Your really finished wingshot, however, utilizes both systems of shooting when and where the demand for either is made. Such a shooter is not met up with every day in the week. Such a shooter will usually perform creditably in the field, whether the game hunted is grouse, quail, dove, or duck.

Your out-and-out approximator will frequently fall down when it comes to dove and duck shooting. The out-and-out aimer, on the other hand, will frequently find himself outclassed in good grouse or woodcock cover.

Although there are plenty of exceptions to prove the rule, you will generally find the aimer a methodical type of shooter; and in the same way, generally speaking, you will find the approximator rated as a fairly fast shot. The kingpin of them all, the natural shot, can shoot in either style. As an illustration, I have seen a hunting companion flush a pair of grouse almost simultaneously and catch his first bird almost before the gun touched his shoulder, taking it clean with a well-centered load just an instant before it dipped over a stone wall—yet swinging calmly on the second bird out in the clearing with all the precision of the rifleman, and bringing it down cleanly with a methodically-aimed shot at a good 45 yards.

As to which type of shot you eventually turn out to be, whether an aimer, an approximator, or a combination of both, I hope nature will have been kind enough to endow you with the potential skill of the latter. But in all probability you will be either an aimer or an approximator, either one or the other; because probably not more than three gunners out of a hundred are born with the lucky combination of qualities that eventually make the fortunate possessor a good performer with the scatter gun either on or off the Skeet field, and particularly on grouse and quail in dense cover, as well as on duck in open, high and fast-flying shooting. And perhaps three out of a hundred is a too-generous estimate at that.

Substantially, the aimer is the shooter who consciously aligns his gun on the flying target and consciously allows for lead or forward allowance. The approximator, on the other hand, is the gunner who depends to no small extent on the magic wizardry that can lie in a pair of well-trained hands. In short, the approximator has learned in large measures to depend with confidence on the accurate performance of a lightning-swift cycle that, aroused at the sight of the target, flicks through his whole being, from eye to trigger finger, with the speed of a whip-snap.

However, never confuse such speed with hurry. There is absolutely no more hurry in such a gunner's performance than there is "hurry" in the maneuver of a striking snake. Let's call it speed with deliberation. Because deliberation always remains the reliable, controlling "governor" on the "engine."

As a beginner, however, you should understand that the progression is in the order named; that is, one should begin as an aimer. Only in the conscious observance of alignment and lead, or forward allowance, can the hands receive the training which eventually may develop into the sub-conscious technique of the so-called snap shot. Don't imagine for a moment that, simply because you throw your gun up quickly once and smash the target, that this makes it self-evident that you have discovered a short cut to becoming a good snap shot.

Almost every youngster, either on the Skeet field, or in the game field, has been thus emboldened beyond reason to imagine that he was really getting somewhere—fast—with his shooting. The youngster may thus be led to suppose he can pursue his shooting education with seven-league boots—but let him take care. Much time may be wasted in that direction. Learn to aim carefully, even meticulously, at first. Allow for forward allowance as carefully as if you were measuring the distance between two points with a tape measure. Slowly but carefully you will develop the beginning of a wingshooting mechanism which may ultimately lead you to the heights you aspire to. But don't try to hurdle your way to the hoped-for destination, because you can't beat the game.

Don't imagine for a moment, either, that snap-shooting must always be lightning-fast—nor ever let yourself in for trailing that other foolish will-o'-wisp, that you can "shoot from the hip" as effectively as you can shoot with your gun at shoulder where it belongs. Learn to aim—to know almost exactly where your gun is pointed at the instant you touch off the trigger. Only by this method—when you miss—will you have established a point from where you can work either backward or forward in your calculations for correction of the fault.

Missing by shooting *behind* the target is by far the commonest fault of the beginner on the Skeet field. Missing by making an *error in elevation* is the commonest mistake of the good shot on the Skeet field. As a beginner, you will make both errors—plenty of them. But your initial problem will be to learn how far to lead your target, or how much forward allowance to give it, in order to keep from shooting behind it—and in this respect, it is probably true that the single-alignment gun (like the autoloader, pump gun and over-and-under) makes forward allowance easier to measure accurately in the hands of the conscious aimer.

On the other hand, I have always felt that, because of the wide horizontal sighting plane offered by the muzzles of the side-by-side double gun, that this type of gun helps the shooter adjust for elevation somewhat more accurately. Logically, it should work out this way. But admittedly, the twin muzzles of the side-by-side double gun cover a lot of territory in the region of the flying target—and thus may not always be best suited to the style of the conscious aimer when it comes to gauging correct lead, or forward allowance.

I have digressed purposely in the foregoing to give the beginner sufficient background before making a choice of any one of the several types of guns commonly used on the Skeet field. The reader may wonder just why I have recommended the side-by-side double gun in 6 to 6½-pound

Mrs. Fay Ingalls, of New York and Hot Springs, winner of the Woman's Skeet Championship at Hot Springs, Va. Others in the squad (left to right) are Fred Markley, of Staunton, Va., Sterling Morton, of Chicago, and Douglas R. Nichols, of New Jersey.

Last year's Lordship and National Woman Skeet Champion — Miss Patricia Laursen, of Akron, Ohio, probably the most graceful Skeet shot in America.

Miss Laursen winning the Great Eastern Woman's Championship.

weight and in 20-gauge for the beginner. I have done so because the side-by-side double gun is definitely superior to either the autoloader or pump gun in the matter of balance and handling quality. The side-by-side double gun may truthfully be said to come closest to "handling itself." More than a century of very careful thinking on the part of our best gun-makers, both here and abroad, have gone into the design and resultant balance of the side-by-side double gun. The autoloader and pump gun, by comparison, are rank newcomers. Indeed, it is well-nigh impossible to envision any such miracle as would succeed in incorporating into either autoloader or pump gun the same balance and handling quality that is inherent in every well-made double gun of the conventional side-by-side type.

So I advise the beginner to start in with a 20-gauge side-by-side double gun of 6 to 6½-pound weight—not only because of the favorable weight and recoil factors, as far as unaccustomed muscles and nerves are concerned, but also because the beginner will be less inclined to fight and struggle unfamiliarly with this gun—which comes nearer than any other type of smooth-bore to doing for the young shooter what he has not yet learned to do for himself.

THE COMPENSATOR

However, if you choose to start in with the favorite weapon of the big-time Skeet shots, then go ahead and buy the autoloader in any gauge, 20, 16, or 12. If you are as wise as you should be, don't get it with barrel in excess of 26-inch length. Also, have a Cutts Compensator installed on the muzzle-end. I would recommend having the Compensator installed in 25-inch over-all length with Skeet tube attached, except that resultant increase in muzzle blast in 25-inch over-all barrel length with this attachment is frequently disturbing—particularly in a gun bigger than 20-gauge.

[35]

In the Cutts Compensator lies another good reason for the top-flight Skeet shooter's pet choice of the single-barrel repeating gun—for it is only on the single-barrel gun that the Compensator can be installed.

The Compensator is a rather widely misunderstood muzzle attachment. That it is an extremely homely appliance cannot be denied. However, there is no use getting finicky about such matters in connection with either the autoloader or pump gun. Neither gun is exactly a thing of beauty— although their appearance of stern utility (and their moderate cost) makes amends for certain shortcomings in aesthetic value, at least to me, and in the eyes of other practical gunners, too.

The Compensator was originally designed to reduce the firing recoil of the military rifle, particularly the semi-automatic military type. Rapid fire could be delivered accurately from such rifles only when recoil was so reduced (by the Compensator) that the weapon would not be jumped out of alignment by the force of the kick. It did not take shotgun shooters long, however, to discover that the application of the Compensator to the shotgun meant the removal of the real *bête noire* of shotgun target shooting. The smart rap of the standard trap load has kept many potential enthusiasts from the 16-yard trap game. Of this I am convinced. Yet trapshooters have never taken to the Compensator, for some reason or other. The Compensator clicked with Skeet shooters right from the start, however—until today, a top-flight Skeet shot in the big matches is hard to find who doesn't use a Compensator on the muzzle-end of his autoloader or pump gun.

There existed an erroneous belief in an earlier day, which persists even yet in some quarters, that the Compensator in some way or other gives an enlarged pattern—that is, larger than the 12-bore cylinder gun. This is not true. The Compensator does not enlarge standard cylinder patterns, therefore gives no such advantage as extra diameter of pattern to the shooter who is using it. The Compensator does, however, give an *even* cylinder pattern, due to lateral escape of gases through its ports, or vents, instead of letting these gases blow ahead into, and more or less disturb, the shot load in its initial flight from the muzzle.

But aside from the definite advantage the Compensator confers in reduction of recoil, the next and possibly the most important of its advantages is the fact that it supplies (with its enlargement at the muzzle) an easy eye-catcher for the shooter to use in making quick and accurate alignment on the flying Skeet target. Curiously enough, when the writer pointed out this advantage, in an article which appeared some years back in *Field & Stream,* Colonel Cutts wrote us that we had "apparently discovered an hitherto unsuspected virtue of the Compensator." Be that as it may, the Compensator's aid in making quick and accurate alignment was proved by the author's experiments with his so-named "Muzzle Bandage" for the single-barrel gun and also with his well-known "Bev-l-Blok" sight for the side-by-side double gun. The latter being a large flat-top Patridge-type front sight for the double gun which acts as a quick eye-catcher, in the same way that the Compensator functions on the muzzle of the single-barrel gun.

The disadvantages of the Compensator are two-fold. Of one disadvantage we have certain proof every time we stand alongside a user of the Compensated gun. This disagreeable feature is its noisiness. Installation of the Compensator necessitates cutting back the length of the barrel. Thus, if we have an over-all barrel length of 26 inches with Compensator installed, the barrel itself is only about 22 inches long. This causes added muzzle blast. This noisiness is somewhat annoyingly apparent to shooters standing near the gunner doing the firing. If the Compensator-equipped barrel is reduced further to 25-inch over-all length, muzzle blast (particularly from the 12-gauge) may be distinctly disagreeable.

However, many excellent Skeet shots go to the shorter 25-inch Compensator-equipped barrel. They stuff their ears with cotton—as every wise shooter does on the Skeet field anyhow—and find the fast-handling short "Compensated" barrel a decided factor in making higher scores in hotly contested competition.

As for the beginner, I recommend the Compensator-equipped autoloader or pump-gun barrel of 26-inch length —no shorter, no longer—and of course with over-all length measured with Skeet (or so-called "spreader") tube attached.

The other criticism I have to make of the Cutts Compensator—although I can't prove it—is that occasionally (I believe) a shot pellet escapes from the tightly-wedged load in emerging from the barrel, strikes the vanes or vents of the Compensator at the wrong angle and emerges as a missile dangerous to other shooters' eyes. I myself have been hit on three or four occasions when standing almost immediately back, or slightly to one side, of the shooter. However, my eyes are always protected with shooting spectacles, so nothing more serious has resulted than the stinging prick of a small pellet, several times necessitating use of a pen-knife blade for removal from the skin. On those few occasions, when I have been standing in this particular position, I doubt seriously that the pellet could have ricocheted from the oncoming target. In fact, examination of one No. 9 pellet that struck (and stuck) in my forehead when shooting on the Camp Fire Skeet range one day seemed to confirm my suspicion that it had slipped through the vent of the Compensator, rather than ricocheted from the oncoming hi-trap station-8 target.

Many shooters use the Compensator on the Skeet field over quite a period of time without realizing fully wherein this muzzle attachment proves of greatest benefit to their shooting. That the Compensator's usefulness in reducing recoil effect is a matter of major importance in clay-target shooting, this was generally recognized, of course. Also, the superior cylinder patterns made with the Compensator offered another obvious reason why scores invariably improved after the shooter's gun was equipped with the device. But I do feel that my recognition of the quick eye-catching quality of the Compensator's enlargement at the muzzle of the shotgun revealed for the first time, in its true significance, an advantage of major importance—as has since been proved by thousands of shooters who have used the author's "Muzzle Bandage" idea on the single barrels of their repeating shotguns.

Further recognition of the importance of this eye-catching enlargement at the muzzle of the shotgun may be seen in Winchester's adoption of the Compensator as standard equipment. By the time this book is published, I have been informed, Winchester will not only have brought its new autoloading shotgun on the market, but will also sell it with Compensator ready installed—at the buyer's option, of course—following the shrewd example already set by the Savage Arms Corporation. And in addition, I believe Winchester also plans to accentuate the Compensator's eye-catching quality along lines suggested by the author's "Muzzle Bandage," as a further aid to the shooter in developing quick and accurate gun-pointing and therefore better timing in wingshooting.

Winchester (according to present plans, I understand) will improve the Compensator's advantage in this direction by enamelling the back part of the Compensator (that part visible to the shooter's eye) either white, or yellow. (They suggested white—we suggested yellow.) According to present understanding, this improvement will be patented and exclusive with Compensator-equipped Winchester guns through the author's release of all priority rights in connection with his "Muzzle Bandage" idea, as outlined in *Field & Stream* for July, 1935.

I might add here that not only will the Winchester autoloader be so equipped, at the shooter's option, but also any other Winchester repeater—such as the well-known Models 12 and 97 pumps and the .410-gauge Model 42. We have pointed out to Winchester that we regard yellow the better color for enamelling on the rear of the Compensator, be-

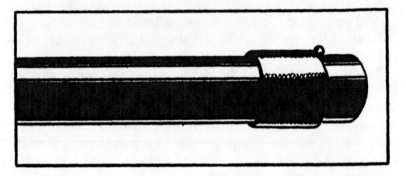

cause science has long since proved that yellow-and-black represents the color combination having highest visibility. Yellow is definitely a better color than white, for instance, against the sky; whilst against the darker woodland, field and thicket, yellow has at least equal visibility, if not better than white.

Before closing on the subject of the Compensator, I might mention that an added advantage of this muzzle attachment on the Skeet field arises from the fact that it provides slight extra weight at the muzzle, therefore makes for a steadier-holding and steadier-swinging muzzle; also that it tends to influence the gunner to shoot slightly lower than he would with a gun with lighter-weight muzzle. This is all in favor of higher scoring on the Skeet field, where the target must always be considered as a *falling* target. This is one of the major differences (of which there are many) between field shooting and Skeet. For in the field, the bird starts from zero speed and steadily accelerates to maximum speed, usually in rising flight; while on the Skeet field the target starts from the trap at maximum speed and flies in downward trajectory to a stop. The Skeet target's trajectory rises only for a short distance (relative to the gunner) before it begins its downward curve under the pulling force of gravity.

All of the foregoing, together with what is to follow, makes this chapter on the selection of the gun seem unduly long. However, full and complete discussion of the gun is fully justified by the important part played on the Skeet field to-day by the rather special gun most perfectly adapted to the game. In this respect, even though I have expressed a preference for the medium-weight 20-gauge side-by-side double gun for the beginner's initial experience, I raise the question myself whether the newcomer to Skeet might not be better counseled right from the start to go to, say, a Compensator-equipped 20-gauge autoloader (or 16-gauge) with 26-inch barrel, barrel length of course measured over-all, with so-called "spreader" tube screwed into the Compensator. The fact that the Compensator can be installed only on the single-barrel type of repeating shotgun offers a second sound reason why this particular gun ranks top choice among Skeet shooters today.

RESPONSIBILITY FOR MALFUNCTION

That the autoloader leads all the other types of guns in popular preference among Skeet shooters is also due to the fact that no manual operation is required during the shooting function. This is important—because, from the beginning of Skeet up until the autumn of 1938, responsibility for malfunctions of the manually-operated pump gun was placed entirely on the shoulders of the shooter. Malfunc-

tion with the pump gun was regarded as "man failure"—
and so charged against the shooter's score. The autoloader,
on the other hand, could malfunction—but here the responsibility was classified as "gun failure," so that the shooter had
a repeat chance at his target without being penalized with a
scored miss. As late as the summer of 1938, during the Lord
ship matches, I witnessed the unfortunate loss of the Lordship Championship by Mr. Lowrey Booth of Chicago, who
easily had the Great Eastern All-Bore crown in the palm of
his hand—until he suffered a single "lost" on his 97th target
through nervous or otherwise incorrect manipulation of
his manually-operated pump gun.

The Skeet rules with reference to pump-gun malfunction
have been eased up considerably since then. The easement
was particularly noticeable at the National matches held
later in September of the same year at Tulsa, Oklahoma.
Also, it would seem only fair to ease the rules with respect
to the pump-gun malfunction, since there are thousands of
shooters who far-and-away prefer to use this standard and
most popular of all American shotguns in all of their shooting, both in the field and at Skeet.

This has been a difficult point to settle. In my mind there
is still question as to whether the matter has been equitably
disposed of even yet. Curiously enough, we seldom hear of
the out-and-out pump-gun shooter losing shots in the game
field through so-called malfunction of his manually-operated
pump. Possibly malfunctions do occur and we don't hear of
them. From personal experience with this excellent gun in
the field, I am inclined to believe that under game-shooting
conditions the pump-gun malfunction (that so frequently
occurs on the Skeet field) is almost non-existent. It is the
tension of modern high-pressure Skeet competition that
causes the pump-gun malfunction—and for this reason I
doubt that it deserves to be called a gun malfunction at all.
It's a man malfunction. The shooter, under tremendous

[42]

tension in a big match, occasionally fails to give the pump gun's action its full backward stroke. His arm muscles are too tense. He anticipates the double shot—something he somehow doesn't do in the field. He tries to work too fast in his doubles shooting—and this is where the trouble always occurs. As a result, he brings the pump-action back on approximately a three-quarter stroke, then starts it forward—then most likely realizes his mistake and slams the action back to its full length—upon which his loaded cartridge ejects from the action and his breech block slams home on an empty chamber. Thus the malfunction with the pump-action—ninety-nine times out of a hundred.

There has been criticism, even, that *deliberate* pump-gun malfunctions have been performed by quick-thinking shooters who, noting that they have scored a miss on the first target of a double, then attempt to go into an intentional malfunction—after which they hope to claim immunity under the rather loose interpretation of the present confused rule on this type of malfunction. I can hardly hold with the view that this unsportsmanlike practice has actually occurred. Nevertheless, it could be possible—and, after all, extreme possibility must always be taken into consideration in drafting laws and rules governing any highly competitive sport.

THE PUMP GUN

From the foregoing, however, the reader will easily see for himself why the pump gun would appear to be a poor choice for the beginner at Skeet—*unless* the beginner happens to be merely a beginner at Skeet, not a beginner in shotgun shooting. If the shooter is accustomed from experience in the game field to handle the pump gun on feathered game, it is assumed he uses the pump gun from choice and therefore in all probability would do his best work with the pump gun on Skeet targets.

Several thousand correspondents write to me each year requesting advice on the purchase of a new shotgun. Most of these letters, as might be supposed, come from men who rate in the medium income bracket. Naturally, interest is mostly centered in low-to-medium-price guns. Also, as is the rule with the majority of young gunners going into the game-shooting field, they seem to be interested most frequently in low-cost double guns.

The tentative buyer of the low-cost gun should understand why it is possible for him to get definitely more gun-value per dollar in buying a single-barrel repeating type of gun in preference to the cheap side-by-side double gun at approximately the same price level. Double guns, with more or less exact twin-tube alignment, are more expensive to make. It costs more to put them together. The single-barrel repeater, on the other hand, costs less to make by reason of the simplicity of its construction. It is, therefore, a simple matter of arithmetic to foresee that the buyer of the single-barrel repeater usually receives definitely more gun-value per dollar in the approximate forty-dollar price class, than he receives when buying a double gun in the same price range.

Certain possible exceptions to this general rule must be noted in all fairness. For I regard the Fox Sterlingworth double gun, selling at about the forty-dollar price range as an excellent buy for the money. Also, for those who want single alignment in the double gun, only two guns are available in the medium-price range among the over-and-unders of this type—the Marlin and Savage—both of which are not only good, serviceable guns, but are surprisingly well balanced, considering the low price asked for them. Yet, not one of these twin-tube low-price guns is the equal, in actual gunmaker's value, of either the Remington Model 31, the Ithaca Model 37, or the Winchester Model 12 pump guns, which cost only three or four dollars more.

The reader may draw his own conclusions—and act accordingly—in the light of the foregoing information. Or, instead of calling it "information," let's merely call it the author's personal opinion. But if for one reason or another, the reader should prefer the twin-tube type of gun, and nothing else will do—then of course he will get his best dollar's worth, as far as he and his personal preference are concerned, by buying either the side-by-side double, or the over-and-under, in the medium-price range, in preference to the pump gun—which latter, for several good and sufficient reasons, he may not prefer.

Among the pump guns most favored on the Skeet field today, it is probable that the Winchester Model 12 holds the edge, through "priority," or seniority. I mean—it seems to me that the Winchester Model 12 holds its edge probably more because of the fact that it is the oldest modern pump gun on the market, with the unimportant exception of its venerable predecessor, the Winchester Model 97 hammer gun. In other words, the Winchester Model 12 is seen more frequently, probably because the man who uses it has been shooting this type of gun over a period of years—no doubt having begun his wingshooting experience with this well-known Winchester hammerless pump in the game field, where it has for some years held a high place in the esteem of hard-bitten field shots and wildfowl gunners who like this reliable standby for its sturdy construction, excellent balance and faultless performance.

A pump gun that has been coming to the front with rapid strides, however, is the Remington Model 31—and this pump gun, in the author's estimation, is the finest trombone repeater in use on the Skeet field today. Its action is smooth and lightning-fast. The soft "hump" of resistance to the backward stroke in the M31 action is just enough to require sufficient pressure to drive the action all the way back in full and complete stroke, once the gunner starts it. By contrast, the action of the Winchester Model 12 is not nearly as smooth. The weight of the Remington Model 31 is excellent for the Skeet field—though for the game field we prefer the lighter-weight Ithaca Model 37, the action of which is the same original John Browning design which Remington once made in its excellent 20-gauge Model 17 and later (for what reason I don't know) obsoleted. In the design of their actions, however, the Ithaca Model 37 and Remington Model 31 pump guns are scarcely unlike enough to be regarded as less than practically identical. Let's just say that they are distinctly similar—both, of course, deriving from John Browning's original design, as first produced in the early 20-gauge Remington Model 17 pump gun no longer made.

(As this book goes to press, Ithaca announces a 5¾-pound 20-gauge Model 37 that is identical with the old discontinued Remington Model 17—thus making the Ithaca M37 available in all three gauges, 12, 16 and 20.)

As mentioned previously, we do not recommend the selection of a pump gun for the beginner on the Skeet field—at least not for the beginner in shotgun shooting who has had no previous field experience with this type of manually-operated repeater. But if for any reason the shooter elects to purchase the pump gun as his preferred Skeet field weapon—here we recommend that his choice be guided in the order named: First, the Remington Model 31, because of its superb action and good Skeet-field weight; second, the Ithaca Model 37 for its (almost) equally superb action; third, the Winchester Model 12 for the unquestioned excellence of its strong design and earned and deserved reputation in the game field, covering more than a quarter of a century.

The Winchester Model 97 is out of the running as far as the Skeet field is concerned—or, perhaps we should say, as far as the beginner in Skeet shooting is concerned. But for those occasional gunners who arrive at the Skeet field for their initial baptism of fire, and who come carrying their trusty Model 97 hammer guns, it would be nonsensical for them to discontinue using their 97's. As a matter of fact, the experienced game shot who has gone through years of eminently satisfactory usage with the soundly designed and well-balanced Model 97 pump, usually wouldn't trade his old smoke-stick for any modern pump gun on the market. And I must say I feel much the same enthusiasm for this hearty old standby, in spite of its heavy "box-car" action—for the old gun is so pleasingly stocked and balanced that it seems to come to (the familiar) shoulder as no other more-modern pump gun does, even today. Also, this is the only pump gun made with visible hammer—a feature which many of its admirers would never be without in a field gun.

THE OVER-AND-UNDER

When it comes to the double gun, which many prefer today for one reason or another, I foresee a steadily growing popularity for the over-and-under. I went on record several years back as predicting that the over-and-under type of gun would rapidly take advantage of the tremendous potential popularity it has in the American market. I made this prediction simply on the basis of the fact that the vast majority of American gunners have grown up with the typically-American single-alignment repeater. Also, most of us have grown up with the .22 rifle—another single-alignment gun. In fact, as a nation of shooters one might say we are "single-alignment minded." Therefore, any type of shotgun which offers the sporting equivalent of the standard side-by-side double gun—and which also makes it possible for us to utilize the principle of single alignment with which we are so familiar—such a gun is bound to advance tremendously in popular acceptance within the next decade or two.

I recall today that it was but a scant few years back that the over-and-under type of gun was only an excessively expensive foreign importation, well beyond the means of the average American gunner. The fine old gun-room maintained by the now extinct New York firm of Von Lengerke & Detmold always kept a few over-and-unders in stock, mostly of German Greifelt make, just as a matter of policy. One could always find in the gun-room of this famous old establishment—which had the atmosphere of a gentlemen's club, rather than a commercial shop—the entire gunning world in review, from the humble pump shotgun and .22 rifle of the average American, up to the costly hand-made smooth-bores of Birmingham and London, as well as the heavy express rifles of Africa. Imported over-and-unders were priced at scarcely less than five hundred dollars, and from there on up to well over a thousand. As a buyer, the typical American gunner, accustomed to the single alignment of the pump and autoloader, had not yet been foreseen in the tremendous potentiality of his market. However, a shrewd American gunmaker was not far in the offing—and the Browning Company soon led the way to the real over-and-under market comprised of millions of American single alignment shotgun shooters. Browning placed on the market the first American over-and-under—though more correctly this over-and-under was not American at all, being made (and still being made) in Belgium, though assembled (as it is today) here in the U.S.A.

The Browning over-and-under was such a success—both from the standpoint of its excellence as well as its quick acceptance in the American market—that it wasn't long before the Remington Arms Company came knocking at the doors of American gun buyers with their over-and-under Model 32. One finds it scarcely necessary to comment on the fine quality of both of these single-alignment double guns at this late date. Both are popular favorites on the Skeet field today, with those who prefer the balance of the double gun combined with the single-alignment advantage of the single-

[48]

barrel repeater. And in the preference of trapshooters, I think the supremacy of these two guns is established beyond question today—that is, in 16-yard doubles shooting.

Both Remington and Browning over-and-unders are available with single trigger. For a while, in its earlier day, the Browning over-and-under was furnished with a foolish and complicated trigger arrangement called a "twin-single" trigger. This was merely the conventional arrangement of double triggers—yet each trigger functioned as a single trigger. Barrel selectivity was achieved in the order in which the triggers were pulled—the front trigger firing under-and-over, while the rear trigger fired over-and-under. The basic idea was to give the hunter in the field instant selectivity, according to the varying range at which game would be shot at —and this idea was sound. However, the "twin-single" trigger represented an attempt to combine too much. Even the best single trigger can scarcely be stretched to cover this extreme in actual field usage. The "twin-single" mechanism was too complicated to prove reliably trouble-proof through the life of the gun. So the "twin-single" idea went by the board—as it certainly deserved to go.

THE SINGLE TRIGGER

To this day, and probably to the end of time, the selective single trigger will offer its slight disadvantage to the game shot in the field—in that it does not make possible instant selectivity according to the requirements of range on flushed wild game. For this reason, many dyed-in-the-wool game shots, who prefer the double gun in the field, either of over-and-under or side-by-side type, still stick to the old-fashioned double trigger. Instant selectivity is possible, in my opinion, only with this old-fashioned double trigger. Also, as far as my personal experience proves, I believe one can shoot just about as fast with double triggers (when occasion demands) as he can with a single trigger. The shift from one trigger to the other takes place during the instant of recoil-recovery from the first shot—at which moment the shooter has ample time for the quick shift of his trigger finger from front to rear, during the momentary interval needed for recovery of alignment from recoil.

Moreover, it is my feeling that the old-fashioned double trigger, of first-grade quality, provides slightly cleaner trigger pull and possibly more instantaneous response to touch-off from the trigger finger than does the average selective single trigger of today. However, this is a small point, of significance probably only to the extremely fussy expert shot.

The single trigger is certainly a boon to the young shot, who, at least in the initial stages of his apprenticeship, would eternally be getting tangled up going from one trigger to the other, between barrels, on the old-fashioned double trigger.

The single trigger offers another important advantage—to the man whose contour of trigger hand, or whose peculiarity of gripping his shotgun stock with his trigger hand, renders him vulnerable to severe bruising on the middle finger, from sharp contact with the trigger guard on its backward jump under recoil. Patented rubber finger guards are effective in certain cases in removing this cause of finger bruising—and the cause should be removed as soon as the shooter's tendency in this direction is noticed. Otherwise a tendency to flinch under the punishment will probably develop, with ruinous effect on the shooter's performance. The better method of removing the trouble, however, is not by means of installing the make-shift finger protector at all, but for the shooter to change immediately to the single trigger—and in such case, a single trigger should be selected which sets well back in the curve of the trigger guard, almost,

Perfect squad formation and movement: The Gilmore Red Lion team, of California, winning the *Field & Stream* Lordship Cup.

Mrs. F. S. Bryan, of Los Angeles.

Mrs. Robert G. Vance, a former Lordship Woman Skeet Champion is also an excellent field shot and prefers the side-by-side double gun.

Mrs. Jean Smythe, of Aurora, Ohio, a Skeet shot of national championship calibre.

if not quite, in the position of the rear trigger in the time-honored double-trigger combination.

It is my frank opinion that there are no finer or more dependable single triggers available today than those supplied as standard equipment on the Winchester Model 21, the Parker and the Remington Model 32 over-and-under. Time was when the single trigger was not expected to be foolproof and trouble-free. But as far as considerable personal experience goes, I am led to believe that the single triggers on these three first-grade American double guns are beyond reproach. At least they have so functioned in my hands over long periods of time.

With respect to the single-trigger mechanism, I might warn the reader at this point not to inject an excessive amount of oil or graphite grease into the "works." In line with the old fallacy that "if one pill is good for you, the whole box ought to be tremendously beneficial" some gunners are inclined to be too lavish in the application of lubricant—which, however excellent in quality, can be used excessively—to result in that most annoying malfunction of the twin-tube shotgun—doubling—that is, both barrels letting go almost simultaneously. The only upsetting experience I ever had with a first-grade single-triggered side-by-side double gun, in this particular fault of doubling, came from this cause—an over-dose of good-grade graphite lubricant which if used only in extreme moderation would have resulted in continued satisfactory performance. A thorough cleansing of the action cleared up the trouble at once.

BARREL LENGTH

In recommending barrel length, it seems scarcely necessary to exhort the reader never to use longer than the 26-inch barrel on the Skeet field. There is only one excuse for longer

[51]

than 26-inch barrel length, and this might be in the case of the shooter who is afflicted with that visual defect known as "far-sightedness." This simply means that the lenses in such a shooter's eyes have so flattened, either through advanced years or for other reasons, that he cannot achieve clear focus on any nearby object. Therefore, he must have a little more barrel length than is normally necessary, extended out into that region where his eyes will focus, in order to help him with his gun-pointing. Certainly barrel length should never exceed 26 inches on the Skeet autoloader or pump gun, as the extra length of action supplies at least four inches extra sighting radius on both of these repeaters. However, one of the foremost shooting writers in the country, now advanced in years, tells me that the 28-inch barrel on a pump gun is better suited to the condition of his eyes today, as proved by the fact that he does better work with this length of sighting radius than with any shorter barrel.

For average use on the Skeet field, however, one has but to look about him at any major Skeet tournament to see how the best shots invariably go to short barrel length. One of the finest Skeet shots in the game, who later turned professional, used a Compensator-equipped autoloader with 24-inch over-all barrel length—and the only reason more good shots don't go under 26 inches with the Compensator-equipped barrel is probably because (as previously mentioned) the Compensator installation necessitates cutting back barrel length about four inches, which, in the case of a 24-inch over-all Compensated barrel, would leave only about 20 inches of actual barrel length—which would result in excessive muzzle blast, particularly with the 12-gauge gun.

As regards correct choke for use on the Skeet field, there is nothing finer or better suited to the purpose than the cylinder patterns thrown by the Compensator's so-called "spreader" tube. The double guns, which can't of course be equipped with Compensator, must have a slight amount of choke to avoid the frequently uneven scatter of the true cylinder bore. Our double-gun manufacturers today bore for Skeet-field use what they call No. 1 and No. 2 Skeet chokes. These correspond, substantially, to improved cylinder and modified respectively. There is no excuse, however, for the No. 2 Skeet choke on a typical Skeet gun. The No. 2 Skeet choke is installed in the double gun simply because, up to the present, the Skeet double gun has been designed for dual purpose—for field shooting as well as Skeet.

The ideal Skeet gun of double-barrel type should have both barrels bored improved cylinder, or No. 1 Skeet choke. However, if you already have a Skeet gun bored No. 1 and No. 2, right and left, and you wish to maintain it in its present dual state, as both field and Skeet gun, do not under any circumstances follow the fallacious advice of those who (though they should know better) advise the closer-patterned No. 2 choke always on the outgoing or more difficult target! Use your wider-pattern No. 1 right barrel always for the difficult target. In fact, use the right barrel right around the field, loading singly in the singles shooting; then, in the doubles, reserve the narrower pattern of the No. 2 Skeet choke in the left barrel for the easier incomer.

Remember the foregoing—for the reverse of this correct interpretation is quite generally prevalent and you will doubtless be wrongly advised on this point any number of times. You have only to appeal to logic to realize that what I have told you is correct—so use the opener No. 1 Skeet pattern *always* on the more difficult outgoing target.

RECOIL PROTECTION

There is only one last word I might add on the selection of the gun—and this has to do with the attachment on the butt-stock of various commercial pads designed to absorb or reduce the effect of gun-recoil.

[53]

It is quite all right to use the recoil pad—and certainly the gunner should use a pad if the recoil of his gun seems to punish him unduly. However, particularly in the case of the Compensator-equipped autoloading gun, it seems to me there should not be sufficient recoil to seriously bruise, or even fatigue, the shooter's shoulder and arm muscles, provided his gun stock is of correct length—and provided he is mounting his gun correctly.

It is regrettable that only a few, apparently, of the Skeet shooters who habitually use the Compensated autoloader on the Skeet field seem to realize that this type of gun can be properly conditioned so that it will transmit only a very reasonable amount of recoil. A certain amount of recoil is necessary in the case of the autoloader, to insure positive functioning in automatic ejection and reloading. But it is safe to say that not one shooter in fifty gives the "insides" of his autoloader the attention it deserves. If this type of gun kicks too hard, all lubrication can be wiped clean from the magazine spindle. In this condition the friction ring will grip the spindle tighter and thus reduce recoil. Or, if recoil effect from the autoloader even then seems unpleasantly heavy, the bevelled steel ring may be brought up on top of the recoil spring in the position recommended by the manufacturer for use of the gun with maximum loads. If the extra grip of the friction ring then retards the backward movement of the barrel to such an extent that the automatic functioning of the gun is interfered with, then a little lubricant may be added to reduce the friction. Thus, by humoring and "doctoring" his individual gun, the shooter may do much to lighten his autoloader's recoil, yet at the same time insure its positive functioning. The habit of most shooters of autoloaders, however, is to let the recoil-absorbing mechanism of the gun go from one year's end to the other without any attention at all. Under such condition of neglect, this part of the autoloader's mechanism can scarcely be expected to remain constant in its performance.

As regards installing the Compensator on the autoloader, here the manufacturer of the gun in times past has complained bitterly—that his gun frequently gets credit for malfunctions that are not its fault—that a certain amount of recoil is essential to proper functioning of the autoloader —that the application of mechanical friction to reduce excessive recoil has already been taken care of in the design and manufacture, as the autoloader can regulate its own recoil to a nicety without the added recoil-reducing function of the Compensator—and in this multi-point complaint, the autoloader manufacturer is more right than wrong.

One realizes of course that you can't adjust an autoloader too closely at the factory. Various loads will be used, under varying conditions of temperature, wear and friction application. It is up to the autoloader shooter himself to do more about this than he has done in the past. The autoloader is one of the easiest, light-recoiling shotguns in the world to shoot when it is worked over with a little patience and intelligence.

As regards recoil from the manually-operated pump gun, here of course it's the proper move to put on a recoil pad if your gun pounds you. Curiously enough, however, the pump gun always has seemed to me to have less kick at the butt-end than the double gun, either of over-and-under or side-by-side type. The reason for this is unquestionably psychological. In other words, the pump-gun shooter's attention is so concentrated on the necessity for jacking a second shell from the magazine into the chamber that, particularly in doubles shooting, the recoil of the gun isn't much noticed. For this reason, I frequently advise shooters to go to the pump gun for a "rest" after they have developed an annoying habit of flinching under the pounding of the double

[55]

gun, or single-barrel 16-yard trap gun. Though, of course, the surest cure to resort to, in the case of the man who is flinching badly, is to go temporarily to a lighter-gauge gun.

The only thing I have against the rubber recoil pad is the likelihood of its catching on one's clothing when mounting the gun. The correct way to mount the gun is to slide the butt up along the body and into well-bedded position at the shoulder. I don't like a gun which, because of exposed raw rubber recoil pad, must be pushed out from the body in the mounting and then pulled back into the shoulder, so as to avoid catching and "hanging" on one's clothing. I also dislike a gun with a recoil pad on it, the surface of which has been covered with very slippery leather—although a little sandpaper worked over the surface of the leather in this case will roughen it just enough to prevent that apprehensive feeling of insecure slippage, particularly on the second shot.

Best of all, I like to "shoot against wood"—that is, have no butt-plate on the gun, either of vulcanized or soft rubber—only the end of the walnut stock, and this nicely checkered to add security against slippage. However, I seem to be peculiarly immune to recoil—probably for the very good reason that I seem to catch much of my gun recoil in both hands, therefore having only a part of the gun-kick transmitted to my shoulder. I know I catch recoil in my hands, because after a session of heavy shooting, the following day I note a slight stiffness in my fingers which "tell-tales" the work they have done.

This matter of recoil effect varying according to the individual shooter is also affected to a considerable degree, I believe, by one's shooting form. The flexible shooter who "shoots loose," as the saying goes, feels recoil to a decided lesser degree than the less fortunate brother who shoots in a physical state of tightly-rigid muscles and tensed nerves. It's a curious fact, but true, that when we shoot the shotgun from the position of more or less motionless rigidity, we receive the full shock of recoil effect from the gun-butt. There is no "give" to the muscles, no "rolling with the punch." This is particularly evident when one fires a shotgun at a stationary target, such as I am frequently called on to do in making pattern tests. Under this shooting condition, the 6¾-pound 12-gauge, with only standard loading of 3 drams equivalent of powder and 1⅛-ounce shot charge, fairly rattles one's teeth. Yet as soon as I revert (with same gun and load) to wingshooting on a moving target, with muscles in fluid and flexible motion, recoil effect dwindles to the practically unnoticeable stage.

5

FIT OF THE GUN

~~~~~~

CORRECT gun-fit is simple enough in principle, though somewhat complex in practical application. Many there are who profess to know a great deal about the *ins* and *outs* of correct gun-fit. But few give any real evidence of understanding correct gun-fit by approaching the subject humbly. Correct gun-fit for the wingshooter is a complex subject mostly because it deals entirely with variables. Tiny fractional changes here and there in the matter of stock proportions and general balance can actually alter the whole of the gun's handling quality. Also, the individual is always a variable quantity. He is in an unending state of change from youth to old age. Probably the only outstanding truth in any discussion of correct gun-fit for the wingshooter is that gun-fit is only a close approximation as far as general gun balance and stock measurements go—and even then the gun and shooter must go along together pretty steadily in shooting practice in order to maintain their close relationship.

Correct gun-fit for the beginner is a simpler matter. This involves certain important stock measurements, true. However, average stock measurements are close enough to the beginner to serve the purpose admirably. Of far more importance in the initial stage of the young shooter's experience is the matter of proper gauge and weight of gun. How many thousands of letters have come in to me I'll never know, in which the principal query runs about thus: What is the best pheasant gun? What is the best gun to use on rabbits? What is the best quail gun? In other words, the beginner makes the obvious error of trying to fit the gun to the *game* instead of fitting the gun to the individual shooter who happens to be *himself*.

The best quail gun is the gun you can hit the most quail with, obviously. The best Skeet gun is the gun you can hit the most Skeet targets with. And so likewise for the best rabbit gun, pheasant gun, woodcock gun, or any other smooth-bore instrument designed for wingshooting.

I have always counselled beginners at Skeet, or beginners in field shooting, to start in with a light-weight gun and with light-recoil charges. For this reason, the 20-gauge seems to be an almost perfect selection for the beginner. And this applies not only to the Skeet field, but also to gunning for feathers and fur in upland shooting. Light gun-weight is easier for unaccustomed muscles to handle. Light recoil is easier for unaccustomed muscles and nerves to tolerate. All beginners, therefore, should graduate *upward* from the 20-gauge—that is, go to the bigger gauges only after skill is acquired and only when the bigger gauge seems desirable and necessary for the job at hand.

Usually, however, it is just the other way around. The beginner starts in with the 12-gauge. In later years, when by dint of keeping everlastingly at it he eventually learns to shoot fairly well, then our gunner may "go fancy" on us and turn to the smaller gauges—and in such case it happens not at all infrequently that the pendulum swings wide in the other direction, even carrying the shooter to the 28-gauge and .410-gauge extreme in "sportiness."

It is a pity that more young shooters can't be influenced to see the wisdom of starting in with light gun-weight and light recoil. They would become good shots in much shorter time if they would go about it this way. But they are informed, by their friends and by reading the monthly output of shooting writers, that the 12-gauge has a definite ballistic superiority over the 20-gauge—which of course it has. They read that the 12-gauge 1⅛-ounce shot load will give greater pattern density at any range than any smaller gauge—which also is perfectly true. In fact, the beginner's chief source of trouble lies in the fact that the beginner himself is the last one in the world to get the idea that his poor performance in the field is chiefly the result of his own ineptitude and not the fault of the gun and load.

Most of the shooting market is made up of young shooters and inexpert shooters. The loading companies, in their advertising, know full well the value of proper psychology in making their appeal. Therefore, the great majority of young and inexpert shooters fall easy victim to the promise of "long-range" killing power. Go to any hardware and sporting goods dealer and ask him what shotgun shells sell the best and he will tell you, invariably, that the heaviest "big-bump" loads he can buy are the ones which move off his shelves the fastest.

This of course is not to suggest that the heavy loads haven't their place. Assuredly these heavy loads have a definite place—but only for expert shots. The expert, through years of experience, has become distinctly target-conscious, not gun-conscious. The expert is therefore more or less shock-proof, partly because he is target-conscious and not gun-conscious, and also partly because he has learned to roll with the punch and never suffers under the shock of recoil. At least, the effect of recoil is reduced to minimum as far as he is concerned. But the inexpert shot, and nearly always the young shooter, imagines that if he can just get a full choke tight enough, and a heavy-enough load that will kill at really *long* range, that his own shortcomings (which he is the last to admit, or even suspect) will somehow or other be discounted.

Anyway, to cut this part of the discussion short, the heavy

12-gauge gun isn't the best gun for the beginner—at least, not for the *average* beginner. But after you have profited by the easier "learnability" of the 20-gauge gun, then by all means go to the 12-gauge—if and when you think you need it. And by the time you progress that far in your experience, you will *know* when you need it.

Perfect gun-fit, which includes not only stock measurements but general balance and handling qualities, is the mysterious will-o'-wisp of the shotgun shooter. It used to be said that once in your life, twice if you were lucky, three times if you wore a veritable necklace of horseshoes, you might find (or perchance even own) a gun that fitted you perfectly. And by a perfect-fitting gun, we mean a gun that comes up "square on the button"—such a gun as you can hit with consistently merely by pointing it subconsciously, as one points his finger at a flying target, without looking at the finger at all. Possession of such a gun is the dream of every shotgun shooter.

Though formerly regarded as a matter more or less of divine Providence, or luck, if you came into possession of such a gun, there is no logical reason for supposing that a man can't achieve pretty close to correct gun-fit for himself if he has patience and intelligence enough to do something toward making his dream come true. In fact, all who do have patience and intelligence enough can rather easily go about the business of making this dream come true on the Skeet field—because the Skeet field is a testing ground which can readily be employed for this very purpose—and I think perhaps this is one of the chief benefits that Skeet has brought to the modern shotgun shooter.

Forty years ago, gunners meekly accepted what the gun manufacturers gave them (or recommended) in the way of standard stock specifications. Most American guns of that period were horrific examples of what the field gun should *not* be.

[61]

The American shotgun of forty years ago was designed on the principle that wingshooting was practically the same as rifle shooting at moving targets. Barrels were long. Chokes were tight. Stocks were bent down to absurd "drop." One was forced to *aim* such a gun. One couldn't possibly point it naturally. That good execution was done with such guns is only proof of the extreme adaptability of the human being to odd and unnatural surroundings. All of which proves that a man can actually fit himself to a bad-fitting gun—and do reasonably good work with it. But, contrariwise, he will always do better work—and more pleasing work for himself and all who watch him—when he shoots with a gun that comes nearer to actually fitting him.

In the years before Skeet, those who were able to buy high-priced guns had to be rather patiently trustful of the mysterious hocus-pocus invoked by the expert gun-fitter. Of course, I do not meant to disparage the definite skill of the really expert gun-fitter. Such a man is a very valuable person to know. But such a man does not belong to any particular "school" of thought regarding proper stock fitting. He is pretty much of an individual himself, unquestionably a good shot, and he treats his customers as individuals—and observes their peculiarities closely.

The really expert stock-maker reaches the apex of his art when he is working with a customer who really knows how to shoot. In other words, the expert is the man who is artist enough in woodworking to understand, interpret and actually execute suggestions that the customer himself can make intelligently on the basis of observed personal experience. In this respect, Skeet has proved to be the great revealer of the true requirements of individual gun-fit. Skeet provides the testing ground where the shooter can be observed by expert eyes, and also observe himself—particularly with regard to errors in his form, shortcomings in the fit of his gun, or possibly faults in both directions, which is most usually the case. But in the last analysis, when we understand correct gun-fit as being the closest-possible approximation of a relationship that is made up entirely of variables, here the shooter must of necessity be the most important force for helping himself, as soon as his skill passes the average point and becomes distinctly above-average.

I might add here, too, that Skeet has undoubtedly helpfully guided our gun-makers by definitely placing within narrower limits what they are pleased to refer to today as "standard" stock specifications designed to fit the average shooter.

The truth of the situation in this matter of gun-fit, after you boil it all down, is that gun-fit can never be more than an approximation. Each of us changes from year to year. Sometimes the change is even more sudden, from month to month. Put on ten pounds and you become a different proposition from the standpoint of gun-fit. Grow a couple of inches and the same thing is true. Change from the light clothing of early autumn to the heavier clothing of mid-winter, and again you have introduced a slightly mis-fit condition which must be compensated for in the way you hold and handle your gun—if you are to perform with that gun in your accustomed style.

Of course, a great deal of this change—this difference between what the shooter actually needs and what his gun-maker offers him—is absorbed by the shooter who keeps himself geared to his gun constantly through more or less shooting right through the year. Skeet accomplishes this maintenance of relationship very beautifully. A couple of rounds on the Skeet field each week-end ought to keep a man pretty thoroughly acquainted with his shotgun—that is, so long as his physical characteristics do not change too much.

In this connection, I have been amused on a number of occasions in the past, to receive letters from shooters obviously in their early twenties who were getting badly punched about the nose, where the knuckle of the thumb on the trigger hand was coming back on recoil with damaging effect. Of course this is only a case of the young man continuing to use the same shotgun stock that he used as a boy, six or eight years previously. But you'd think that this possibility might occur to the shooter—and I like to think that on many occasions the young man is bright enough to think it out for himself. Nevertheless, a great many prefer to write the gun editor, inquiring as to the cause of the "mysterious" bad behavior in the last year or two of a dearly beloved gun that had treated them naught but gently through the tender years of their youth!

So you might say with perfect truth that this matter of gun-fit is never a fixed or stationary quantity, or relationship, between the shooter and his gun. But where the shooter uses his gun steadily—and where also he is past the age where he is undergoing any wide physical changes—it is probable that steady practice will keep him and his gun pretty much in tune with each other.

I am of the opinion, also, that the gun-maker and the stock-fitter can go only about so far—and that from there on the individual himself is in best position to achieve the best possible fit between himself and his gun. The Skeet shooter is lucky in this particular, because he has always got the testing ground of the local Skeet field to help him check up the value of any stock changes he might be contemplating. The shooter can make such changes temporary for the sake of test; then if they prove out all right, the next step is to have them duplicated, or crystallized, by the gunsmith, or expert stock-maker.

You might say that in such standardized smooth-bores as our American repeaters, like the autoloader and pump gun, that the average stock specification of approximately 14-inch pull, 2½-inch drop at heel and 1½-inch drop at comb, would result in guns that were identical in balance and handling qualities. Well, they are identical—almost. But within that little word "almost" lies a rich field for exploration by the individual gunner.

The American autoloader and pump repeater, while not possessing the poetry of balance of the finer side-by-side double guns, nevertheless are very easily and economically adaptable to the subtle nuances of the shooter's individual physical peculiarities. The stocks on our autoloaders and pump guns are not only readily adjustable at slight expense, but are also easily replaceable at low cost in case the shooter's inexpert experimentation carries him beyond bounds and results in the ruin of that particular stock. Therefore, we can take liberties in experimenting with such shotgun stocks —and intelligent experimentation frequently leads to very happy and satisfying results.

The man who is short of neck and wide of face can take a piece of glass and scrape down the side of his gun-stock comb, until the extra width of his face and thickness of his cheek is allowed for exactly—and his eye is thus correctly brought into alignment over the center line of the barrel.

Likewise, if stock length seems excessive, he can remove the butt-plate and see if the length thus shortened by ¼ to ⅜ inch brings the gun nearer to the "feel" he is looking for. Or, if the stock seems overly short, he can add a series of two or more thicknesses of pasteboard (cut to the same contour as the end of the butt-stock) to lengthen the stock for temporary experiment—and if the increased length enables him to do better work, then he can have his gunsmith match the wood in lengthening the stock, or perform the simpler job of adding a good standard recoil pad to add ¼ or ½ inch, or more, to the length of pull.

If the comb seems too high he can scrape that down slightly, too, with a piece of glass—though making no change here greater than ¹⁄₁₆ of an inch without shooting the gun for test—nor indeed making any changes *anywhere* without

[65]

shooting the gun for a check-up test during the temporary stage.

One of the simplest alterations on the autoloader or pump-gun stock is in the matter of changing pitch—and from the benefits which I personally have observed as resulting from changes in pitch, I am led to believe that this specification in the shotgun is a factor the importance of which has been considerably under-rated for many years.

As a rule, it is safe to say of most any new autoloader or pump gun that pitch can be slightly increased for best results on the Skeet field. The Skeet target is a falling target, usually a rather rapid-falling target at the time the average gunner shoots at it. So, in a Skeet gun, it is perhaps better for your scoring to have the charge centering about six inches low at 25-yard range, than to have the charge hitting directly "on the button."

In this latter connection, however, I have always been of the opinion that a shotgun for all-round wing and target shooting should center its charge exactly where the gunner *feels* he is pointing it. For many years the Winchester pumps were made to shoot high (still are, as a matter of fact) the better to enable the gunner to catch birds on the usual rise in the field. Such a high-shooting gun might work very well on straight-away, or even on quartering shots. But suppose the gunner has a level-flying 40-yard crossing shot—what of the high-shooting gun then? Change his "hold" to under? Not my way.

This is why I say the all-round (field as well as Skeet) shotgun should center its charge exactly where the gunner feels he is pointing. With such a gun, the shooter himself should know his wingshooting well enough to make necessary compensation, one way or the other, according to the character of his target's flight. But in a gun to be used strictly on Skeet, the slightly low-shooting quality (such as centering the charge about six inches low at 25 yards) unquestionably

Mr. Frank R. Kelly, of New Jersey, calls for the hi-trap outgoer at station 2. Note the fine pivotal control used by this All-America Ace. Observe how his eyes look to the left of the line of his gun to catch the first glimpse of the out-flying target. Thus he sees the start of the target behind his muzzle and his gun has a "running start" in the race to catch, overtake and smash the target.

Dr. Robert G. Vance, of Massachusetts. Both feet in good leverage contact with the ground, weight evenly distributed; yet note slight shift to left-leg pivot for the lo-trap target at station 3, with right leg ready to "follow".

Mr. S. Lewis Hutcheson, New York State Champion, pivots on slightly bent left leg in taking the lo-trap target at station 3, using a variation in application, but not in principle.

offers a scoring advantage not to be ignored. Such a low-shooting quality in a gun serves as a slight extra margin of insurance against risk—on a uniform target in a regimented shotgun game where over-shooting is a common error!

The matter of changing pitch on a shotgun is the easiest of jobs. If you are consistently over-shooting—and if you are reasonably assured your stock is not definitely too straight —I advise taking the gun over to the nearest cobbler's shop and hiring the use of the cobbler's sand-wheel for no longer than about fifteen minutes. Take off the butt-plate and very gently and lightly begin dressing off the toe of the stock. Do the work very gently, very carefully, very evenly—and most of all, very, *very* gradually. Keep testing the gun as you work, throwing it up quickly on a spot on the wall without taking conscious aim by means of the gun's sight. As you throw the gun up, see that it comes nearer and nearer to landing "dead-on" the target spot without need of conscious alignment. Perhaps it will be better for you not to try to do the whole job at one session. Better take the gun out and try it over the week-end—and if there is still a slight tendency to over-shoot, bring it back the next week-end for final dressing off at the toe. But be careful how you work—for a sixteenth of an inch is a "bite" here—and an eighth of an inch is frequently plenty.

After dressing off the toe of a gun-stock, conduct the shooting test without replacing the butt-plate. As a matter of fact, I wouldn't be surprised but that you may find the slightly-shortened stock length not only feels better, but that it may also possibly help you to better scoring. It is my belief (though expressed here with proper caution) that the average man shoots a stock that's a little bit on the long side, at Skeet.

Our British friends would throw up their hands in horror at any such length of pull as 13½ to 13¾ inches. However, most of the English guns are stocked for over-head shooting on driven grouse and pheasant. In this kind of over-head shooting, it is admittedly an advantage to hold the fore-end hand in close to the trigger-guard. Also, the long stock is an advantage. It is distinctly not necessary to hold out far on the fore-end to support and control gun-weight in such over-head shooting. After all, the gun is in nearly vertical, or at least sharply-inclined position, where most of the weight rests on the shoulder under contact from the butt. Some British shooters hold well out on the fore-end, just the same—in fact, I am informed that His Late Majesty, George V, reputedly an excellent game shot, held well out on the fore-end of his gun in this style. This is entirely a matter of personal preference. It is a habit of mine to place my fore-end hand well out on the barrels, away from the trigger-guard. This gives extreme control and leverage advantage in the management of the gun's forward weight. I probably got into the habit of shooting in this style through quite a few years of rough shooting behind a spaniel. It was always necessary for me to be ready to shoot quick—therefore I unconsciously adopted the far-out hold on the fore-end to give extreme leverage control of the gun.

But such extreme control is not necessary on the Skeet field. Here we know exactly where the target is coming from, where it is going to fly, and approximately when it is going to appear. One should probably avoid the too-far-out hold on the barrels, at Skeet as well as elsewhere, as such a hold makes it very easy to stop gun-swing. This, however, is a matter which every shooter must decide for himself. But it is probably best in the long run to adopt an average "all-purpose" hold which one will eventually employ unconsciously in taking any kind of a shot on any kind of game, whether clay target or feathers, yet always the same.

To prove that the length of pull is not nearly as important as some would have you believe, I might point out in the case of the average fine double gun with double triggers that while pull from the front trigger might be as much as 14½ inches, when the shooter brings his finger back to the rear trigger his pull is shortened by a good ¾ of an inch, or more—in which case he is actually shooting a 13¾-inch stock on the second barrel instead of the 14½-inch pull of the gun-maker's specification!

Instead of the standard 14-inch pull usually found on the American autoloader and pump gun, I really feel that the average Skeet shot might perhaps be better suited with a little less length of pull—say not more than about 13¾-inch. Or, suppose we put it this way—that if we must err slightly, then let's err on the short side in Skeet, rather than the long side, as far as length of pull is concerned—and for this reason: The advantage of the slightly shorter stock on the Skeet field is the fact that shortened pull tends to make a lower-shooting gun—and this very well fits in with the Skeet game, where the target is always a falling target and where one of the commonest errors is to miss by *over*-shooting.

Because of the fact that the short stock tends to make a gun shoot low, we can easily see why the typical English game gun, admittedly used most frequently on high overhead in-comers in driven game, should be free from any treatment which would tend to make the gun shoot even slightly low.

Of course, the proper way to use any remedy is not to take the "whole box of pills simply because one of them should be good for you." The truth of the matter is, stocks can be over-shortened to such extreme as to prove a distinct detriment to the shooter's skill. In fact, stock length, or length of pull, should be a finely-balanced and correlated measurement—not so short as to give the shooter too rigid control over his gun and without sufficient command of the sighting radius from breech to muzzle—nor yet too long, so that the shooter might have insufficient control over his gun for quick and positive mounting, the kind of gun-handling that is necessary and advantageous on the Skeet field.

I cannot end this chapter on the correct fit of the Skeet gun, without having at least a word to say about the type of stock-grip I prefer, and why I prefer it.

To be brief, there is only one type of shotgun that may possibly be better stocked with other than the straight-hand grip. This is the pump gun—which logically should (perhaps) be stocked with a modified or half-pistol grip. The only reason the pump gun possibly needs the half-pistol grip is that this grip serves better as a "stop" against having the grip slip forward through the shooter's trigger-hand on the forward "pump" of the trombone action, in closing the action in doubles or "repeater" shooting.

This instance, it seems to me, offers the only plausible excuse for having the so-called "pistol" grip on a shotgun —and a particular abomination in my humble estimation is the *full* pistol grip on the shotgun. Here are my reasons:

The full pistol grip induces a rigidity of hold—whereas just exactly the opposite of rigidity, or *flexibility,* is called for in wingshooting. Rigidity of hold is correct for the target rifle, shooting at a stationary bull's-eye. But to "freeze" on to your shotgun grip—or on to your shotgun fore-end, either, for that matter—this is diametrically opposed to the very fundamental of wingshooting, which is *fluidity*—fluidity of muscular control, fluidity of motion, fluidity of finger, wrist, and body movement. In other words, it seems to me quite as absurd to advocate the need for rigidity in gripping and holding the shotgun, as it would be to preach a need for "rigidity of hold" in using a 3½-ounce fly rod.

The straight-hand grip induces soothing and reassuring fluidity and flexibility in gun-handling. Understand, of course, I am not talking now with respect to rifle shooting —nor with respect to a game like trapshooting, where the gun is already mounted and roughly aligned before calling for the target. I am talking about the only type of shotgun shooting worth talking about—shooting in the field (or

at Skeet) where the shooting function begins from scratch
and includes everything, all the way up from the mounting
of the gun to the crash of the shot.

The straight-hand grip is definitely superior in that it permits more of the shooter's hand to be in light but assuring
contact with the stock in guiding the butt to secure and uniform bedding at the shoulder.

The straight-hand stock also allows the trigger hand to
assume a more natural position—lying extended along the
under-part of the stock—and not only in the gun-down position, but also with the gun-up in the firing position.

The straight-hand grip is also superior in the case of the
two-trigger double gun, in permitting the trigger-hand to
adjust more easily for the shift to the hind trigger on the
second shot in doubles shooting—although this advantage
is rather out-dated in these days of the almost-universally-
used single trigger.

I truly believe that ninety-nine shooters out of a hundred
(except those using the pump gun) will never go back to
any form of pistol grip once they have become accustomed
to the sweet and reassuring "feel" of the straight-hand grip.
Indeed, on such easy-actioned pump guns as the Remington
Model 31 and Ithaca Model 37, I wouldn't be at all surprised
if most shooters of these excellent guns might definitely
prefer the straight-hand grip once they "get over" the disturbing unfamiliarity that comes with initial use of any new
thing.

Oddly enough, we seldom if ever see the autoloader or
over-and-under guns stocked by American factories with
the straight-hand grip. Yet both Browning autoloader and
over-and-under are stocked very generally with the straight-
hand grip for the Continental and British trade.

Another advantage of the straight-hand grip which almost
slipped my mind is the fact that you can always use a longer
length of pull—a longer stock, that is—with the straight-hand

grip. The reason is, that your trigger hand is extended in natural position with the straight-hand grip; whereas with the pistol type of grip the hand is more or less restricted. Although I personally like short stocks for my own use, I do know that sufficient length of stock is desirable—just as too-little length of pull is a disadvantage. But for those like myself, who like the easy-mounting action of the short stock —probably induced by our habit of holding out a little too far on the fore-end—the straight-hand feature offers this additional advantage of *providing necessary added stock length that isn't adversely noticeable.*

6

THE EYES

EYES are the shooter's most precious equipment. You can't shoot expertly if you can't see well. Conversely, the better you see, the better you'll shoot. However, in a regimented shooting game like Skeet, where targets are usually thrown against a sky background, even the shooter with poor vision is not handicapped nearly to the extent that he would be in brush and thicket shooting on feathered game.

Optical glass, in the form of spectacle lenses, is used on the Skeet field in conjunction with poor vision as a corrective. But an equally important part played by optical glass on the Skeet field is as a *protective*. The danger to shooters' and spectators' eyes that lurks on the Skeet field is well-known by this time, or should be. I see no necessity for "preaching" on the advisability of protecting the eyes on the Skeet field, because the shooter or spectator who doesn't yet recognize the hazards wouldn't pay any attention anyway.

Danger to one's eyes from target fragments is a minor hazard today, since we now have the form of Skeet known as "angle" Skeet, where the targets are thrown at an outward angle. In an older day, when the targets were thrown back and.forth on a straight line between stations 1 and 7, the danger from target fragments was much greater. It was quite common to see a man cut about the face, head and hands ten years ago, during the day of "shuttle" Skeet. The only real danger today is from ricochet shot pellets—and this danger is not as great as it used to be.

[73]

Unlike the target fragment, the ricochet shot pellet is so small that the eye can't see it. Therefore the sensitive protective reflexes of the eye never have an opportunity to function in the face of danger from a ricochet pellet.

The small No. 9 pellet, which for some reason or other has been chosen as standard size for Skeet, is a known offender in this respect. Larger-size shot do not flatten and ricochet as readily. Larger shot pellets would not extend the boundaries of the present Skeet field danger zone. In fact, a shot size like 7½ chilled would be most appropriate for 25-yard Skeet shooting. The normal charge of 7½ chilled would insure ample density of pattern. And the use of this shot size would unquestionably reduce the ever-present danger of ricochet "stingers."

What he does with his eyes is strictly the shooter's own business. But we do get a case of "shivers" every once in a while when we see stupid parents allowing wide-open-eyed little children to play around the Skeet field while a squad is shooting.

I wear spectacles on the Skeet field because I have known men who would have lost half their eyesight had they not been wearing spectacles at the time. I have known other men who came perilously near losing an eye from the sting of a ricochet shot pellet when they were not wearing spectacles at all. They were just lucky. One of my very good friends from Kentucky, a crack Skeet shot, was hit just a half-inch under his right eye at the Lordship matches two years ago. The pellet penetrated so deep it had to be taken out by a doctor later on. Yet to this day, this shooter still continues to do without the protection of shooting spectacles—evidently being one of those who believe that lightning never strikes twice in the same place. Providence takes care of some shooters. Luck is a good thing to take advantage of when it comes along and a poor thing to depend on.

I myself have been hit so many times in the face and

hands, not only by target fragments, but also by ricochet shot pellets, that I consider any man, or woman, an almost complete dimwit who ventures on or near a Skeet field, either as shooter or spectator, without his eyes properly protected by well-made spectacles fitted with first-grade lenses of optical glass.

I do not recommend going to the other extreme, however, in wearing what are known as "shatter-proof" spectacle lenses. In the first place, this shatter-proof lens construction is three-ply, two glass layers glued to a non-shatterable core. The net result of this construction, I am informed, is that it slightly reduces visual power. This being true, we may not see quite as sharply through shatter-proof lenses as through clear optical-glass lenses.

Actually, there is no particular need for the added protection provided by the shatter-proof feature. The three-ply shatter-proof construction is not really necessary on the Skeet field. I happen to be quite sure of my ground in making such an assertion. I have worn spectacles from early youth, have been hit in the eye with everything from a baseball to fragments of Skeet targets, yet have never had a lens break into my eye. A spectacle lens of first-grade optical glass will turn a ricochet No. 9 shot pellet—of this I am reasonably sure. But even should the ricochet pellet chip the spectacle lens, the eye's quick reaction in closing would prevent any injury to the eyeball.

We may conclude, that while the shatter-proof glass is quite the proper thing for the automobile windshield, it isn't the best thing to put over your eyes in a shooting game that calls for all the sharpness of vision your eyes can muster. Your eyes will be safe enough behind good-quality ground lenses of optical glass; and you will see better with such lenses.

With respect to adequate eye protection, I know of no better spectacles than those turned out by such high-grade concerns as Bausch & Lomb of Rochester, the American Optical Company of Southbridge, Mass., the F. W. King Optical Company of Cleveland, W. H. Belz, Inc., and Clairmont & Nichols, both of New York—the latter concern having no connection with the author.

Bausch & Lomb and the American Optical Company are manufacturers of optical glass. Their products are of superlative quality. I specially recommend the *Calobar* lens of the American Optical Company—and the same type of lens (identical with *Calobar,* I believe) as furnished by Bausch & Lomb in the *Ray-Ban* spectacles.

Optical glass made by these high-grade concerns is not cheap. The "spectacles" or "sun glasses" you buy in the "notion" stores for fifty cents or a dollar, complete with frames, are usually not fit to put in front of your eyes.

Such cheap spectacles are frequently made of blown glass, more easily shattered by flying missiles such as the ricochet No. 9 pellet, small as it is. Such "lenses" are not particularly good for your eyes to look through—and not at all trustworthy to depend on in case danger threatens.

In the matter of correct lenses for Skeet field use, these should be of two types. First of all, we should have a glass that will protect the eyes against the bright glare of sunlight. Not all Skeet fields can be laid out advantageously facing in the northeasterly direction. Ground conditions are unsuited in the average instance—with the result that only in isolated cases can the Skeet field be ideally located so that shooters' eyes are fairly well protected from direct glare of the sun, particularly under conditions of mid-summer sunlight.

Lenses best adapted to furnishing adequate protection to the eyes from sun glare are the American Optical Company *Calobar* and the Bausch & Lomb *Ray-Ban*—these two being practically identical as far as I can see—also the Belz *Sharp-site.*

Now and then comes a dull day when we need something to brighten up the "field" a bit, so that we can see the targets better. In this respect, along comes the F. W. King Optical Company with the excellent *Rifleite* glass which over a long period of years has established an enviable reputation among shooters everywhere, shotgun as well as rifle and pistol. The chief purpose of the *Rifleite* lens is to brighten up visibility of the target on cloudy, overcast days. The *Rifleite* lens employs the color combination which scientific test has shown to possess highest visibility rating—black against yellow background. The *Rifleite* lenses themselves furnish the brilliant yellow background upon which the black target appears sharp and distinct—and as far as I can see, it makes no difference whether the target is a stationary bull's-eye on the rifle range, or a flying target on the Skeet field. So for a dull day always have in your shooting kit a pair of *Rifleite* spectacles. They will serve you well when you need them most.

Similar to (if, indeed, not practically identical with) the *Rifleite* lens is the Belz *Britesite* lens of canary yellow shade. Equally good, in my opinion.

Another excellent lens which is well adapted to just a medium-bright day—such a day as might alternate between shadow and sunlight—is the *C-Sharp* glass imported into this country by Clairmont & Nichols. This *C-Sharp* is a peculiar glass, with gray or slightly gray-blue cast to it. Happily named, the *C-Sharp* lens seems to sharpen definition and it also brightens colors. An excellent glass I consider it, especially desirable for a day when sunlight is not too brilliant and when cloud shadows don't absorb too much light.

Any one of these leading types of optical glass can be purchased plain, or ground to optical prescription if needed. Your optician can fit them to your spectacles in any prescription your oculist finds necessary. And when it comes to the spectacle frame, I consider as probable top choice the Bausch & Lomb frame recently developed in their well-known shooting spectacle. The F. W. King Optical Company has its own special spectacle frame, also excellent, though slightly better suited to the rifle and pistol range than to the Skeet field.

Now let's go into the more interesting discussion of what our eyes can mean to us as an aid (or hindrance) to good shooting:

It has been said that the shotgun shooter can function with a very fair degree of skill even if his vision is definitely below normal. This is true—to a certain extent. The man with poor vision may still be a good wingshot where his targets are out in the open, against the sky, where visibility is good.

A gunner with medium-to-poor vision may also be a fair duck shot, where birds coming from a distance don't need to be focused on quickly and where the shots are generally taken against the light of the sky. But take this same gunner into heavy upland game cover, such as the woodcock's alder thicket, or in good grouse cover, and he will be pretty much lost.

As far as the Skeet field is concerned, however, indifferent vision, or even downright poor vision need not stop a man from trying. And his perseverance may result in his becoming a quite decent Skeet shot, provided he begins with and gradually acquires the fundamentals of correct shooting form.

It is a foregone conclusion, of course, that the man with indifferent or poor vision will never become a champion. He may become a good Skeet shot—in fact may develop into an excellent Skeet shot. But the man with keen, sharp vision will always hold the edge over him in any competition.

Why do you suppose we see nearly all of the championships in regional and national Skeet competition held by youngsters—and I mean youngsters usually in their 'teens, or seldom beyond their early twenties?

Simply because *young* eyes see better on the average than *old* eyes. And of course there is always the definite certainty that as eyes grow older they become less and less keen.

So while second-rate vision may not actually prevent a man from becoming a good performer on the Skeet field, you can depend on it that this shooter will always be beaten by a man of equal gun-pointing skill who has the extra advantage of better vision. In the game field there is no fair ground for the two to meet on—the man with keen vision will simply "run away" with the less fortunate lad whose eyes are less keen.

As an example of what keen vision can do for one, in making him an outstanding shot, I was most interested this last summer to talk with Mr. Joe Hiestand shortly after this great shot's triumph in completely obliterating the former world's straight-run record on registered 16-yard targets.

It was at the Grand American last summer—where he arrived with an unfinished run of 66 registered targets and calmly proceeded to smash 900 more—that this outstanding gun pointer told me something about his almost perfect vision that made me appreciate more fully the real reason for his amazing skill as a trap shot:

Hiestand apparently happens to be one of those odd freaks of perfection that occur in nature only about once or twice in a century. First of all, he has perfect health and an unruffled temperament. He is not phlegmatic in the usual sense of the word—too intelligent for that—but seems to have all the awareness of a wild thing, combined with the "upstairs" of a highly civilized being. To top it off, he has almost bird-like vision. He can see and be warned in advance of variations in target flight long before these variations become apparent to the average shooter's eye. He told me that he knows almost exactly what a 16-yard target is going to do the instant it shows above the trap. For example—if it shows up as a flat ellipse he knows it will be a flat-sailing *low*

[79]

target. If the ellipse appears a bit less flat he knows instantly that the target will be a slight *riser*. And should the target appear as a really *fat* ellipse, Hiestand's eyes flash the instant signal to brain and trigger finger—*quick riser*.

You can appreciate what an advantage over the "field" Hiestand holds—particularly on a gusty day when the targets (for the average run-of-mill shooter) might prove exceedingly tricky—a condition which could easily induce a feeling of nervous apprehension in the mind of the average shooter.

Because he can see like this, the phenomenal Hiestand is never startled, never surprised by unusual target performance. His eye-to-brain reaction is instantaneous. His coordination from eye to trigger finger is almost super-humanly perfect. His shooting mechanism is therefore never jittered by apprehension. What usually happens is obvious. You can't beat such a shooter so long as he keeps his health.

I mention the foregoing because it offers an outstanding example of the tremendous advantage keen eyesight gives a shooter. Hiestand, incidentally, went on from the Grand last summer to continue his world-record-shattering straight run on registered 16-yard targets. He ran 213 more in a row, raising the mark to 1179, which is nearly twice the former world record that stood unchallenged through fifteen years, from 1923 to 1938.

The next thing on the bill of fare, with respect to the eyes, is that most important factor of *how you see*. If you are right-handed, are you also *right*-eyed? If you are left-handed, are you also *left*-eyed? Or, are you one of those unfortunate individuals (as far as shotgun shooting is concerned) who is either right-handed and *left*-eyed, or left-handed and *right*-eyed—in short, either a crossed-dextral, or a crossed-sinistral?

As to which class you belong in, this will determine your shooting style—perhaps even determine your ultimate skill as far as the Skeet field is concerned.

[80]

Statistics gathered by those who pry into other people's affairs tell us that about 92 per cent of all persons are right-handed—about 7 per cent are left-handed—and about 1 per cent are ambi-dextrous.

If you are right-handed, you ought to stand a fair chance of being right-eyed, too. Being right-eyed means having your *master* eye on the right side. However, there is no absolute assurance that this will be the case. You may just as likely be one of the unfortunates who are definitely right-handed, yet just as definitely left-eyed. About 70 per cent of all right-handed persons are right-eyed, they say—and approximately the same proportion of left-handed persons are also left-eyed.

Of course, there would be little or no need of going into this confusing discussion of the master eye—of being right-eyed, or left-eyed—except that the position of the master eye dictates to a large extent whether you will ever be able to shoot a gun in the style known as *binocular* shooting—that is, shooting with both eyes open.

To be right-handed and right-eyed—that is, to shoot from the right shoulder and have your master eye on your right side—this is a very happy state of affairs as far as your wing-shooting is concerned. This classifies you as a straight-dextral and you will be able to shoot with both eyes open with little or no practice to accustom yourself to the decidedly advantageous trick.

On the other hand, if you are left-handed and also definitely left-eyed—that is, if you shoot from the left shoulder and have your master eye on the left side—here again you are fortunate. In this equally happy circumstance, you are classified as a straight-sinistral—and you, too, will be able to shoot with both eyes open with the greatest of ease.

Some authorities claim that the ability to shoot binocularly, with both eyes wide open, is an acquired trick. Maybe so. In the case of the *marked* straight-dextral and the *marked*

[81]

straight-sinistral, I doubt it. For this fortunate twain, binocular shooting comes almost as naturally as breathing. For all others, binocular shooting is probably an acquired trick—and may even be an impossible trick to accomplish in certain cases.

One of the most difficult problems in wingshooting, as far as the eyes are concerned, is encountered in the shooter who is either a crossed-dextral, or a crossed-sinistral. The crossed-dextral of course is right-handed and left-eyed—that is, shoots from the right shoulder but has the left master eye. The crossed-sinistral is, oppositely, left-handed but right-eyed—that is, shoots from the left shoulder but has his master eye on the right side.

Of course, the whole business would be of no particular significance—except that there is no question at all but that binocular shooting is the right way to handle a gun on flying game—or flying targets. Nature gave us two eyes to see with, the better to judge distance and perspective. Also, it is very unusual to find a man who can shoot with style and real flash in the field on feathered game unless he does shoot with both eyes wide open. I know what I am talking about here —I myself am a crossed-dextral and shot for years in the field by partially closing or "winking" my left eye just at the instant of pulling the trigger. Good shooting can be done— mighty good shooting on occasion—but it will seldom show the real "class" of first-rate binocular work.

Binocular shooting, however, is not absolutely necessary in clay-target shooting—such as in 16-yard trapshooting, or on the Skeet field. Here there is no surprise element—we know exactly where the target is coming from, where it is going and about when it is going to appear. Skeet shooters, therefore, can very well shoot with one eye only—and as a matter of fact, quite a few excellent Skeet shots do shoot with the off-side eye closed, or "winked." However, shotgun shooting of this sort can never be as much fun as when you

In position to hit anything that flies, from almost any direction. Typical of the good field shot. Note slight weight shift to left leg for left-quartering lo-trap target at station 5. Mr. Doak Roberts, of Texas.

Many top-flight shooters prefer bending the pivot leg and keeping the counterbalance leg more or less straight—as does Mr. Alex Kerr, shown here calling for the lo-trap left-quartering target at station 5.

Mr. Junior Baldridge, of Indiana, calling for the lo-trap target at station 3. Note that weight is correctly pivoted to left leg for this left-crossing target.

shoot with both eyes open. I know. I have been on both sides of the fence.

As a crossed-dextral I shot with one eye "winked" for many years. Then I changed over and actually trained myself to shoot with both eyes open, without changing my gun to the opposite side. It took me two years to turn the trick, and I'd estimate about ten thousand shells. Whether others, similarly maladjusted, might be able to do the same, this I don't know. I wouldn't advise trying it. My experience was simply an interesting laboratory case to me—a challenge to me to see whether I *could* learn to shoot with both eyes open. So be fore-warned.

Even today, if I dwell for more than an instant on the gun, my left master eye asserts its latent mastery and pulls the muzzle into a cross-fire—which scores a miss. I must always be on guard against "riding" a target or paying more than a minimum of attention to the gun. This personal experiment—particularly its more or less successful termination—has afforded me quite a bit of pleasure and satisfaction. However, in all probability I'd be a better shot today had I used the same amount of time and effort in drilling myself to handle the gun from the opposite shoulder.

Changing one's gun-handling from one side to the other should not be a terribly difficult feat for the boy or young man. But it really is difficult to accomplish once one is past thirty—and may be well-nigh impossible to make such a change past the age of forty. However, "impossible" is a horrid word—and my enthusiasm for *genus homo* is so boundless, in spite of all his woeful shortcomings, that I am unwilling to warn him away from any goal with a word that he has proved silly and meaningless, time and again.

I handled my own case as I did, simply because I am intensely right-handed. Today I represent a curious topsy-turvy right-and-left mixture. For example—I shoot the rifle from the right side preferably and close the left eye in aim-

[83]

ing. Yet, in the prone position, I can make better scores shooting the rifle from the left side and shooting with both eyes open. I shoot the handgun preferably from the right hand, shoot with both eyes open and aim with the left eye. I can shoot the handgun also from the left hand, but here again aim with the left eye with both eyes open. Finally, I wing-shoot with the shotgun, using the gun from the right shoulder and shooting with both eyes open—here keeping most of my vision concentrated on the target and very little devoted to the gun and its alignment.

Regardless of the fact that there are some very good Skeet shots who close or "wink" the off-side eye in shooting, I urge the shooter by all means to cultivate the binocular method of shooting *if* he is definitely a straight-dextral, or definitely a straight-sinistral. Learn binocular shooting if you can—because it is the best and certainly the most enjoyable way to shoot. Nature has given you two eyes, the better to estimate speed and distance accurately. You will always see more clearly and in more nearly correct proportion with both eyes wide open. Therefore, let no one tell you to use only one eye in wingshooting—if you are definitely a straight-dextral or a straight-sinistral.

In the case, however, of the crossed-dextral or crossed-sinistral—here I say most emphatically, take either one or the other of two choices: Either (1) change your gun over to the master-eye side—a change that isn't particularly difficult to make in the earlier years of one's life, although it comes increasing difficult past the age of thirty-five; or (2) shoot from the shoulder that feels most natural to you and close the off-side eye—or only partly close or "wink" it—just before swinging ahead of the target and pulling the trigger. I know good Skeet shots—and game shots, too—who use both methods.

Where the shooter is really interested in the Skeet field as a wingshooting laboratory—and particularly interested in

making the most of his own potentialities as a wing shot—
then Skeet offers a most excellent experimental laboratory.
In fact, it has been in this sense and in this direction that I
personally have enjoyed Skeet most.

Finally, become a binocular wing shot if you possibly can.
For I am convinced from my own experience, that only with
the binocular shooter does wingshooting become really
thrilling, most highly pleasurable and artistic. Also, as between two shooters of otherwise equal skill, I am equally
certain that the binocular shooter will always be the better
all-round shot—and there is no question but that he will win
hands-down over his one-eyed opponent in the field, particularly when it comes to thicket and brush shooting.

But I almost forgot— How to determine which is your
master eye? That's easy. Take an ordinary paste-board mail-
ing-tube—or roll up a paper tube out of a sheet of paper.
Hold it out at arm's length straight in front of you and look
through it with both eyes open—centering it on a spot on
the opposite wall. Now close one eye—then the other—and
determine which eye was doing the looking *through* the
tube. This test will instantly reveal to you whether it's your
right, or your left, eye which is master.

7

FORM AND STANCE

G O about the country today, from east coast to west coast, and watch Skeet shooters perform whose scoring ability rates all the way from just so-so up to top-notch. After observing the shooting "form" of about 97 per cent of our Skeet shooters—if you are ignorant of wingshooting and the principles of form requirements, you may finish your watching in a sort of bewildered haze. You may observe very little suggestion of what nearly two centuries of wingshooting experience has fundamentalized.

The principal reason for this "Tower of Babel" among average Skeet shooters—this apparent lack of a common, fundamental form—is due to the fact that Skeet is a new game. Skeet shooters imagine that Skeet's very newness represents wingshooting conditions which have not existed before. Actually, the solid principles of wingshooting have been firmly established for much more than a century—and the application of these principles to the ultra-modern game of Skeet is not only logical and natural, but unavoidable if one is really to understand the game and properly to go about learning to shoot it.

Skeet is simply shooting at moving targets. There is nothing new in this. Moving targets have been shot at for a long, long time, and the principles which men learned through trial-and-error experience and close study of the problem in nearly two centuries of shooting on moving targets with the shotgun—these same principles apply to Skeet today, just as they have applied for years and years to the shooting of flying game in the field.

But go about today—watching Skeet shooters ranking all the way from mediocre to good in skill—and it might come quite logically to you, the novice, that the correct way to shoot Skeet is to adopt a grotesque body position, sometimes twisted almost into pretzel shape. Nothing could be farther from the truth. We have the pretzel stance, the bowlegged stance, the squat stance, and many other mongrel interpretations of what good stance ought to be—and we have all these weird variations of what should be correct wingshooting stance principally because Skeet is a *young* game.

Because Skeet is young, the public generally clothes it in more or less mystery. I imagine much the same thing was true in the earlier day of ordinary 16-yard trapshooting—that even this old shotgun game was "interpreted" by early devotees as requiring a variety of peculiar postures and weird shooting positions.

Two or three decades hence, we may expect our Skeet shooters to stand more nearly upright and to shoot in the form that has been proved universally correct under any and all conditions for shooting at moving targets. But for the present, our Skeet shooters will continue, at least for a while, in the belief that the intricacies of Skeet demand peculiar (and sometimes startling, to say the least) treatment.

The chief reason why we note so much bad shooting form on the Skeet field today is that the average Skeet shooter is usually apprehensive over his ability to kill the flying target. This apprehension is clearly evidenced in the painfully crouched position, which spells apprehension with a capital A. Such a shooter forgets (or has no clear idea of) the fundamental principles which definitely open the way for fluid muscle movement and easy follow-through in all wingshooting.

The disadvantageous stance commonly used by the average Skeet shooter may also be due to the fact that the shooter is attempting to handle gun-weight slightly beyond his strength—sometimes quite beyond his strength. Thus we mark frequently the widely-separated feet, the contorted crouch, the tensed muscles, all of which are plain tell-tales that the shooter, apprehensive, is subconsciously seeking extra leverage power for the movement of excessive gun-weight. This is unquestionably the result of wide-spread usage of the 12-gauge autoloader—which certainly represents more gun-weight than the average non-athletic individual can handle in fast, easy and effortless style.

Can the shooter whose performance has become firmly entrenched in bad form ever readjust himself to the fundamentals of good form? It is almost doubtful. That is why getting started right is so important. Once a man gets into the rut of bad form in his shooting, he will arrive, later or sooner, at the point where he is more or less proficient at the business of target busting. Confidence in himself has been built up during the period in which he has acquired his peculiar, or even bad, shooting style. Therefore, should we attempt later to change the style of such a shooter, we might seriously undermine his confidence in his own ability. Any subsequent bad showing in his shooting would immediately be damned by him as an indictment of correct wing-shooting principles. In short, it would be difficult indeed to convince him that his bad shooting form is incorrect. And because he can score consistently in his bad shooting form, he will more than likely scoff at your plea for adoption of correct principles of wingshooting. Being human, he naturally goes on the theory that the test of the pudding is in the eating. His ugly, ungraceful shooting form enables him to break a fairly high percentage of his targets. He half-heartedly tries your suggestion for better shooting form— and, true to his expectations, scores below his accustomed skill. Therefore, your way (unquestionably the *right* way) is forever after nothing but applesauce as far as he is concerned.

Another reason why we see so much poor form on the Skeet field today is that the average Skeet shooter is something of a show-off. This is less widely true today perhaps than ten years ago. But it has always been true—and it always will be true in a new game. In shooting a new and unfamiliar game—with possibly a few onlookers on the sidelines—your shooter makes an effort to give plenty of visual evidence to the gallery that this is really tough work and something very special in the way of a shooting spectacle that he is providing. I happen to know the "top-side" functionings of the average Skeet shooter fairly well, having been "one of him" for more than a dozen years, from the beginning of the game up to the present.

How well do I recall back ten years ago how we used to "lay it on thick"—particularly at station 8. You should have seen the anguished squatting, crouching, and all the terrific concentration of nerve and muscle! When we smashed the station-8 target there would come from onlookers that nervous titter of incredulity that indicated the gallery's acceptance of such performance as being little short of Herculean.

Young games are like that. Also, young shooters can be like this when entering games that are not so young. I recall driving through the rural mid-western country one summer not so long ago—and stopping off at a Sunday trap shoot where the boys were holding a match to establish temporary supremacy among a small group of local "hot shots." Of all the curious and awe-inspiring interpretations of "correct" trapshooting stance that were paraded for the edification of the onlooking public that day, one lad in particular "took the cake." First of all, he turned his cap around 180 degrees, so that the visor sloped down the nape of his neck instead of shading his eyes! Then he crouched in almost kneeling position, with left knee cocked out in front and right leg stiffly extended straight behind him. He looked as though he were on his "mark" waiting for the bark of the starter's pistol. Oddly enough, he did a pretty fair job of shooting. Unquestionably he felt he had discovered the ultimate, the very last word in 16-yard trapshooting form. You could tell it by the triumphant gleam in his eye. I wonder whether he ever got much better than the 91 he shot that day. I never saw him again.

Skeet shooting is a very young game. Trapshooting, on the other hand, is an old game. In the early days of trapshooting I have no doubt many odd and individual conceptions and "interpretations" of correct form were observable at every trapshooting meet. But today, at the Amateur Trapshooting Association's Grand American tournament at Vandalia, Ohio, each summer, observation of the top-notchers in the game reveals that oddities in stance, or variations from accepted shooting form, are noticeable chiefly by their absence. Take the Joe Hiestands, the Ned Lillys, Walter Beavers and others in the top brackets, for example. You see these shooters standing upright, with feet placed fairly close together, left foot comfortably out in front of the right in the case of the right-handed gunner—and you never hear them call "pull" in anything but a modulated, non-disturbing tone. No bellowing. No trick calls. No acrobatics. But deadly shooting!

From the foregoing, you can conclude that wide-spread poor form among Skeet shooters today is due principally to the fact that the game is a young and somewhat untutored bumpkin—and that Skeet shooters of the future should give a far prettier picture of wingshooting skill on the Skeet field. Our present-day shooters are generally using guns of too-great weight—and this, together with natural apprehension induced by a somewhat new target-shooting game, makes them reflect the tension they feel (and show) in their labored form and stance.

Good form in any outdoor sport is always good to look at—

though this is in no sense the foremost reason for acquisition of good form.

Good form is a widely misused and much misunderstood term. Good form in wingshooting, for instance, is never a matter of useless, pompous artificiality. Good form in wing-shooting encompasses the basic fundamentals, the hard and fast essentialities which experience has taught bring the best results. Therefore, good form is absolutely without relationship to artificial frills or to silly-ass posing—in short, is based on simple axioms that practical game shots have learned through the greater part of two centuries of gunning over upland and marsh.

Good form is a fundamental principle that we should try to adhere to as closely as possible. Not all of us can be graceful shots, more the pity—for the simple reason that very few humans there be who are truly graceful in any of their movements. But none of us—unless we are so unfortunate as to suffer from extreme physical imperfection—needs to be a grotesque performer with the scatter gun, as too many shooters are on the Skeet field today.

Good shooting form on the Skeet field is easy to acquire and easy to apply—for the simple reason that on the Skeet field we always know exactly *where* the target is coming from, about *when* it will appear, as well as the *direction* of flight.

Good form in wingshooting on feathered game is more of a catch-as-catch-can system, with every man for his own side and Devil take him if caught flat-footed. Particularly is this true over here in our American style of rough shooting—though in England, with game driven into the line of guns, and with each gunner standing at ready on ground previously prepared for secure footing—here more attention may be paid to the subtler niceties of what one may call really good shooting form. Less excuse, I might add, can be found for what is distinctly poor shooting form under such ideal gunning conditions.

[91]

Essentially, however, good form in shooting, whether on the Skeet field or elsewhere, is simply the application of principles that others through years of experience, in the firing of thousands of cartridges, have found resultful of better scoring. Therefore, it is a good plan for each of us, in beginning this game of Skeet, to try to mould our shooting form along lines that have proven sound in the experience of others through more than a century of gunning.

Good form, far from being affectation is really *adaptation*. To try for good form right from the start is to take the common-sense view that wing shots, through more than a century of trial-and-error method, have possibly learned something of value that it might pay us to try out for ourselves. Granted that one is an original thinker—nevertheless, it's only smart to check against the experience of others.

Good form is universal in its application—and far from being complex is actually the essence of simplicity. Good form on the Skeet field means simply—elimination of lost, wasted and useless motion—and consequently the elimination of awkward, unbalanced and ungraceful strain.

Shooting in good form, we not only shoot better, but we enjoy ourselves more—and what's more, we look as though we are enjoying ourselves more.

In this connection, nothing was more pleasing to shooters' eyes than the picture of Miss Patricia Laursen winning the Great Eastern Women's Championship at Lordship in the summer of 1938. This charming 17-year-old girl handled her shotgun with beautiful ease and picturesque grace—and shot with as deadly precision as the hardest-boiled male contestant. When she won, her final shot was greeted by the most vociferous and spontaneous burst of applause I have ever heard at a major Skeet match—which indicated that shooters can and do appreciate graceful shooting, just as they appreciate good scoring.

By training ourselves in the idea of good form, from the

very beginning, eventually we are also relieved of much of the anxiety and apprehension that leads to violation of Skeet's rule No. 3—on gun position. Certainly, any removal, or even reduction, of nervousness and apprehension will tend to make us better Skeet shots. So you may conclude that, while good form on the Skeet field may make us more pleasing to behold, and possibly more of a credit to a pretty gun-game, by far the most important advantage to the shooter himself is the practical certainty that *good form will make him a better Skeet shot.*

We have already mentioned how excessive gun-weight frequently induces incorrect stance on the Skeet field. The average shooter with heavy 12-gauge autoloader often makes the mistake of holding the gun out from his body while waiting in the ready position for the appearance of the target. Why any shooter believes that it is easier to overcome the inertia of the gun's weight with practically the whole of the gun's weight extended outward from his body, this I cannot answer. Overcoming inertia of the gun's dead-weight is a vital matter in the initial movement of mounting the gun—make no mistake about that!

From long years of practical experiment it has been found always easier to overcome the inertia of the gun's weight when the gun itself is held fairly close-in to the body—where initial movement imparted to the gun is mostly upward and under the stronger leverage control of the shoulder-to-forearm muscles.

Judging only from the countless thousands of very passable golfers we have in the United States today—I should say that if the real secret of correct stance on the Skeet field ever becomes suddenly revealed (as we hope this book may reveal it) we may see thousands of excellent Skeet shots appearing in our midst almost within a single season. For the principle of stance that is correct on the Skeet field is so identical with the principle of stance that is correct in golf, that it is really amazing the striking parallel hasn't been made use of already by more shooters. Yet practically all Skeet shooters, even those who should know better, apparently prefer to think of Skeet as something decidedly different and in no way related to the weight-shift and pivotal control so familiar to the good golfer.

Just because Skeet happens to be a gun-game, about ninety-nine out of every hundred people regard it as something decidedly different and apart. Yet the pivot and weight-shift, alternating from one foot to the other, applies in Skeet, generally speaking, just as it does in golf.

On the left-crossing target, the gunner must always use his *left* leg as the pivot leg—while his *right* leg acts as pusher, counter-balance and follower. Conversely, on the right-crossing shot, here the gunner must shift his weight to the pivot of his *right* leg—in which case his *left* leg immediately assumes the role of pusher, counter-balance and follower.

On the straight-away target, the right-handed gunner pivots his weight on the left foot. This is pronouncedly the case with the target coming overhead from behind and going away at the time shot at—such a target, for example, as Skeet's station-1 outgoer. Here the weight-shift to the left foot tends to pivot and free the downward swing of the gun in the vertical plane and in the path of the target—for such a target must be *under*-shot to be correctly led and hit—though not necessarily *consciously* under-shot.

On the high target coming in overhead, here (for the right-handed gunner) the weight shifts to the *right* leg, while the *left* leg takes up the function of pusher, counter-balance and follower—for here the upward movement of the gun barrel in the vertical arc of swing must have no restraining muscles or anchored body-weight to retard or check its follow-through.

From the foregoing, the reader will perceive that correct

form (in Skeet, as in golf) rests on the fundamental principle that *the body in movement must never be a house divided against itself*. In short, there must be a coordinated unity to body motion—which is just a highfalutin definition for *automatic follow-through*.

You can see, therefore, how unfortunate it is for the beginner at Skeet to receive the kind of amateur coaching he usually does get in his initial attempt at this very simple wing-shooting game, with targets thrown from two trap houses 40 yards apart on a 21-yard-radius firing line. If I should seem overly critical of the usual well-intentioned instructions given by amateur "experts" to the beginner on the occasion of the latter's initial effort, it is only because patience wears thin at the repeated spectacle of the self-elected coach invariably starting *the cart before the horse*.

For example, you who have had the "benefits" of amateur coaching may recall that you were told to lead thus-and-so on each given target—and above all, to follow through on each shot.

Well, first of all, nobody can tell the personal *you* how far to lead. You can be told the correct *mathematical* lead for any given target, true. But beyond that it must be a simple problem of trial-and-error—*for you alone to solve*. Even after you become a good shot, you will discover that your swift approximation of lead may actually vary from day to day—sometimes even from morning to afternoon. In the case of the expert shot, however, this variation is seldom more than slight.

As you grow older, after twenty to thirty years' experience, or more, in wingshooting, you may possibly arrive at the conclusion that correct lead, or forward allowance, has little or nothing to do with mere linear units of feet and inches—that, instead, correct lead is a mysterious product of Time and Motion which, in the absence of a clearer definitive, we simply call *timing*.

In the matter of achieving correct follow-through—I will say here and now that if all of us had to depend on cerebral function and *voluntary* action to acquire the habit of following-through on each shot, that there could be no consistently good shots on the Skeet field today. Correct follow-through with the gun-swing must be involuntary, subconscious—*and such automatic follow-through can be achieved only by standing correctly and by pivoting the weight correctly in swinging on each target.*

You have doubtless heard frequently the exclamation from a shooter that such-and-such a target was "missed by a foot." I will go farther than that—will say that ninety-nine times out of a hundred when a target is missed on the Skeet field that it is missed by just exactly *two feet*. And by "two feet" I do not refer to 24 inches linear measure, but to the incorrect placing of the shooter's two pedal extremities.

In short, if your two feet are placed correctly, your lead, gun-swing and follow-through are effortless and automatic. If placed incorrectly, you may miss by "two feet"—exactly.

When the shooter follows the fundamental principle of standing so as to pivot correctly (smoothly and under perfect control) in the direction of target flight, he is bound to follow-through as naturally as night follows day. Stand right and you don't need to think about follow-through. Stand wrong—and it makes no difference how much you concentrate on following-through, your bound-up, resisting muscles will hamper and retard gun-swing as sure as death and taxes.

In the chapters that follow, you will learn more about the simple mechanics of correct stance and resultant automatic follow-through, with absolute "ball-bearing" freedom of unrestrained muscular fluidity.

8

THE "MINIMOVE" METHOD

~~~~~~

SHOOTING ahead of a flying target, in order to inter-
cept it in full flight with an accurately-directed charge
of shot, is a simple piece of mechanics that is quite
widely misunderstood—and what's more, quite widely mis-
interpreted to beginners at wingshooting by those who
should know better.

At the risk of being called dogmatic, I am going to tell
you here and now that there is only one correct and preferred way to do this trick. This right way is to swing on
your target from behind—then race your gun-muzzle past
the target and fire at an instant when your sense of timing
tells you you are far enough ahead of the target to do the
trick.

I realize that you have probably been told before this
that it is a good idea to get your gun ahead of the target and
then swing along with a more or less "maintained" lead,
while you "study the situation" before letting off the shot.
But I have only to say this—that any older shooter who
would so advise a young shooter to adopt this laborious
method of leading the flying target, simply reveals himself
as one who has little or no conception of the *art* of wingshooting.

A man who leads his target laboriously by swinging his
muzzle ahead of the target—and then letting muzzle and
target travel along together while he "ponders" or esti-
mates correct lead—such a fellow will never be anything

but a slow, poking shot. Colonel Peter Hawker very well expressed his feeling (and my own, too) toward such a wing shot in his *Instructions to Young Sportsmen*, wherein he wrote, many years ago: *"Such is my opinion of the slow, poking shot, that I would rather see a man miss in good, than kill in bad, style."* Amen!

To swing on the target from behind, to swing past the target and shoot almost in the same instant, this is the only way to develop a sense of timing. A sense of timing, I might add, is just about all there is to good wingshooting. Strangely enough, there are those even today who think that there are three different methods of leading employed by (1) the gun-swinger, (2) the half-snap shot, and (3) the snap-shot.

Actually, all three methods of shooting start from the same fundamental method of coming from behind the target, swinging past it and firing. The deliberate gun-swinger illustrates this style in its primary stage. The man who half-snaps illustrates the same method somewhat speeded up in timing. While the pure snap-shot illustrates the same identical method of leading, only done at maximum speed. In other words, this is all one and the same method—the first being "public school"—the second "college"—while the third is distinctly "post-graduate." And the proof of this is that any first-class shot is capable of performing in all three styles of shooting—whereas he couldn't possibly be capable of mastering and using at will three separate styles, except that they all three operate on one and the same fundamental principle.

The purpose of swinging on the target from behind—always from behind—is to get your gun-muzzle first of all into the plane of the target's flight. This is what we call establishing elevation. The second reason why we should come from behind is that by racing the gun-muzzle past the target we actually measure the speed of the target's flight. Our "inside" shooting mechanism thus gains a good, close estimate

Mr. Jack Horton, Rhode Island, twice National Junior Champion 99x100 and 100x100, calling for the hi-trap outgoer at station 2. Correct weight shift to right leg for right-quartering target especially noticeable in stance of left-handed gunner.

Some shooters prefer to sacrifice leverage control and shoot with feet close together, even in actual contact, as demonstrated by Mr. Charles King, crack shot of Texas. Where normal pivotal shift from one leg to the other may be confusing to the shooter, this method of pivoting from the central column of both legs close together is perhaps preferable. A slight crouch will help such a shooter overcome inertia of heavy gun-weight; stance better suited to management of medium-to-light gun-weight.

of how much swing past the target will be required to hit dead center. After this curious sixth sense is developed, the target can go past us like a streak—or it can travel at a more leisurely pace—yet our trained sense of timing will come close to telling us exactly how much "push" to give the swinging gun-muzzle in order to have it catch the target with a dead-centered load. Of course, you won't develop and crystallize this fine sense of timing in a month—maybe not in less than five years—but eventually it should become a part of you.

Your first attempts at leading should probably be attempted in the rather laborious "measured" style of the slow, poking shot. That's ABC stuff—primary but necessary. But if you keep in mind the necessity for approaching nearer the true conception of art in wingshooting, you will unconsciously progress from the slow, "measuring" style to the rapid *sub-conscious* method of flipping your gun-muzzle through to correct lead without thinking why or how you do it.

It is wise, here, to caution the beginner at wingshooting that he should probably use the slower and more laborious "measuring" method of leading at first. But it is also wise to give him an encouraging picture of the real art of wing-shooting, which he will come into later on as a natural progression from the slow and laborious method of approximating correct lead on the flying target.

Much has been written on the subject of effecting follow-through in the gun-swing. Practically nothing is mentioned with regard to the vital significance of stance, or body position, in its relationship to *maintenance* of gun-swing. Yet if you are standing correctly—so that your muscles don't get in each other's way and counteract each other's movements—maintenance of gun-swing is practically automatic. In fact, when you stand correctly it is almost impossible to stop gun-swing!

[99]

By standing correctly, let's get it firmly fixed in mind right here—that in all wingshooting, either one leg or the other must act as pivot; and with one leg acting as pivot, the other leg always functions as pusher, counter-balance and follower. Keep that axiom in mind—it's worth much more than its weight in gold.

Recognition of this principle is the sum and substance of what I refer to as the *Minimove Method*.

Let us illustrate how this matter of body balance affects the whole wingshooting function, from gun-mounting to establishing lead and firing—and in describing this principle we shall refer exclusively to the right-handed shot:

In wingshooting, just as in golf, in order to achieve free-running muscular motion we must hinge all movement in a given direction on a pivot—then let the body's weight follow-through in the direction of movement. Thus, in shooting we must pivot on the *left* leg for the left-crossing shot—and pivot on the *right* leg for the right-crossing shot. Also, on the over-head incomer, here the shooter (right-handed) must pivot on the *right* leg—and on the over-head outgoer, here he must shift his pivot to the *left* leg.

All you have to do to convince yourself of the utter truth and soundness of this principle of pivot and follow-through, is to take your gun and demonstrate to yourself that this is true. Your own gun will tell you!

Of course, the shooter can apply the principle variously. You can shoot either from the open stance—with feet rather widely separated—or from the closed stance, with feet quite close together. It makes no difference at all, so long as the variation offers no violation of the *principle*. With the feet close together, in the closed stance, the weight-shift will be quicker and less noticeable—but here the shooter will sacrifice a certain amount of leverage control. Of course, you may not mind sacrificing a bit of leverage control if you are using a light gun—but you will be at a disadvantage with a heavy gun—and the most favored gun on the Skeet field today, among the better shots, seems to be the very heavy 12-gauge autoloader.

However, I don't favor either extreme. I think the feet too close together, in the closed stance, sacrifices too much leverage control. I also feel that the overly-wide stance, with feet rather too-widely separated, while it gives powerful leverage control for the management of excessive gun-weight, still it is not as flexible as that compromise which I call the intermediate or *normal* stance.

Normal stance for the average man (and still considering only the right-handed shot) means carrying the left foot slightly in advance of the right, with heels probably not more than about 8 to 10 inches apart. Stand this way with your gun in hand, just for a test—to demonstrate to yourself how correct is this principle of shifting weight from one leg to the other, or vice versa, according to the demands enforced by target flight. Mount your gun and swing to the left as you would on a left-crossing target—and you will feel your body weight shift naturally to the *left* leg—and you'll also feel the right leg responding naturally, functioning in its capacity as pusher, counter-balance and follower.

Without changing the position of your feet, now swing on an imaginary right-crossing target and feel your body weight shift to the *right* leg—whereupon the *left* leg naturally "comes along" faithfully to fulfill its useful and natural function as pusher, counter-balance and follower.

In the same way, try swinging your gun on an imaginary target coming in high overhead—and again feel your body weight shift naturally back to the *right* leg, while the *left* leg acts as cautious lifter, counter-balance and follower in steadying your aim and putting you in strategic position to give that fast upward flip to your muzzle that is so necessary to kill on this kind of a shot.

And again, to complete the demonstration, take the high

over-head target going away—and here feel your body weight shift to the *left* leg, with the right leg naturally following-through in its steadying effect as pusher, counter-balance and follower.

I roughly approximate correct relative distribution of body weight as being somewhere in the neighborhood of 55 per cent on the *pivot* leg and 45 per cent on the counter-balancing follower leg. Maybe a 51–49 percentage relationship would come nearer the truth. Or 60–40, for that matter. This will probably vary with the individual—and will surely vary according to whether the shooter uses the "open" or "closed" stance. Let the reader experiment with himself here —and hold fast only to the *principle*.

Because there is no opposed muscular effort encountered in this correct system of pivoting and following-through with body weight—obviously there is no lost motion. Avoidance of lost motion means that every bit of muscular effort is functioning at maximum efficiency. There is no conflict between muscular function to introduce error. You can see easily why I call this system the *Minimove Method*. For it is simply a method of minimizing and rationalizing the movement of body and gun weight—a method which eliminates useless and opposed forces which introduce error.

Start your gun swinging after the target on the correct principle of the *Minimove Method* and involuntary follow-through comes along as a perfectly natural and subconscious sequence. How stupid in the past to exhort the beginner "not to forget to follow-through." As if follow-through were a quality which could be "remembered" and consciously applied during the shooting function!

Actually, any approach to correct shooting principles must invariably be made by way of the sub-conscious. Show me a shooter who has to "think" where to hold on each shot, as it is presented, and I will show you a misser, not a hitter. On the other hand—show me a shooter who has a coordinated sub-conscious *will to hit* and I will show you a crack shot under any or all conditions, today, tomorrow, this week, or next month—barring illness or accident. It's smart to do your thinking—but never while you're going after the target.

The Skeet shooter who has trained himself in the principles of the *Minimove Method* should never be forced to resort to that foolish practice of mounting and aiming his gun three or four times at an imaginary spot before calling for his target. Using the *Minimove Method,* all you want to be sure of is that your feet are correctly placed and that your weight is correctly distributed pivotally—then dare the target to come out!

I have always thought that the average shooter taking three or four practice aims at an imaginary spot over station 8 makes one of the silliest pictures on the Skeet field. I have even done it myself—and felt silly doing it. First of all, it's an admission of uncertainty. Second, it burns up nervous energy—in certain temperaments might considerably increase tension and build up apprehension.

Also, such foolish preliminary "aiming"—while it does encourage the habit of killing the target uniformly within a certain area—actually means that the shooter is more or less off balance when he momentarily turns away from this spot to face the trap and the appearance of his target. You can say that he "uncoils" to former shooting position in time to kill his target at the chosen "spot." Nevertheless, this habit of momentarily swinging himself off center is not entirely correct in principle—regardless of the fact that not a few good Skeet shots employ it and seem to succeed in spite of its extremely doubtful worth.

How different to shoot at the same target according to the principle of the *Minimove Method.* In the natural stance induced by the *Minimove Method* there is no off-center or unbalanced position in the whole arc of swing. The body's

[103]

weight distribution, pivoting and follow-through function as naturally as water flowing downhill.

Also, not the least of the advantages of the *Minimove Method* is the fact that you have no mental "tightness" due to the feeling that you must smash your bird within your selected "spot" area. The principle of the *Minimove Method* enables you to smash your target at any point within a rather generous arc of swing—though the development of your timing mechanism (under the more correct *Minimove Method*) will result eventually in your killing your targets very uniformly before they travel more than 18 to 23 yards from the trap.

In this latter respect, the *Minimove Method* may lead some critic of the future to describe it as a "spot" shooter's formula. However, you can readily see that the *Minimove Method* simply favors the development of a system of uniform and subconscious timing. In short, operating on the principle of the *Minimove Method,* the timing of your shot becomes more and more automatic. No need to think of it. Conflicting and opposed muscular reactions are out of the way. The track is clear for smooth and accurate gun-swing in the path of target flight—and once started you *can't* stop it.

There should never be any difficulty in applying the principles of the *Minimove Method* to singles targets on the Skeet field. The beginner has ample time to adjust his position most advantageously before he calls for his target. Let him position himself with care—so that he is sure he has selected the proper foot for pivoting in each case. Drilling one's self in applying the *Minimove* principle to each singles target on the Skeet field is advisable, also, in dry-shooting exercise. One can practice this at home. Such dry-shooting practice may pay excellent dividends, later, under actual shooting conditions.

In the doubles shooting, here the beginner may get mixed up occasionally under actual shooting conditions on the

Skeet field. But eventually, he will fall into the best possible shooting position as naturally as a spaniel takes to water.

It is my feeling that the *Minimove Method* of correct pivotal control of body weight will probably be grasped in a shorter space of time by the man or woman who is a good golfer. The similarity of principle will be instantly appreciated—and although application of the *Minimove Method* applies exclusively only to Skeet, the golfer will at least recognize an old and invaluable acquaintance, even though the latter may be decked out in only faintly familiar habiliments.

9

LEAD, OR FORWARD ALLOWANCE

NOW comes the ticklish part of wingshooting—the lead, or as the British more correctly refer to it, the forward allowance. Be it said right here that no one can tell you exactly how much to lead a flying target —that is, how far ahead of the target you have got to aim in order to have your shot-charge reach the target at the same time the target reaches the spot where the shot pattern ought to be centered.

Thirty years ago, when we luckless beginners didn't have the excellent testing ground of the Skeet field to teach us the rudimentary facts of wingshooting, we were constantly led astray by the varying recommendations of seasoned game shots. Some hunters would tell you to lead a duck ten feet. On a famous Long Island ducking marsh there was a good-natured quip among club members, that "if ten feet seems too much lead, try twenty." Occasionally, a game shot whose performance in the field commanded your respect would tell you that he didn't lead his birds at all! Such a shooter may have been perfectly honest—undoubtedly was—simply because he didn't realize that he was leading without knowing it. Invariably, such a shot was a crack performer in the field—usually at his best on fast short-range work in thick cover. Aim and lead would be such a rapid and instinctive function in his case that he probably honestly didn't realize that he was actually pulling ahead of his birds before his trigger let-off.

The fact is, every flying target must be led. The reason is plain arithmetic. It takes a certain fraction of a second (1) for your eye to tell your brain to shoot; (2) for your brain to tell your trigger finger to pull; (3) for your trigger finger to snap home; (4) for the hammer to fall; (5) for the primer to explode the powder charge and send the shot-charge hurtling on its way; not to mention (6) the fraction of a second required for your shot-charge to travel the 20, 30, 40, or more yards between gun-muzzle and target. All this takes time. Very little, to be sure, but remember that the bird (or target) in the air isn't standing still either. In short, your shot-charge must start toward a point that is *ahead* of the flying target and *in its path*.

Only experience will teach the young gunner where this point is for varying types of targets. It will be farther ahead on a down-wind teal duck going past at express-train speed. It will be less for a lumbering pheasant cackling up out of the swamp—though don't make the common error of thinking the pheasant is a slow-flying bird when he really gets under way—because he is actually a fast mover, and this coupled with the fact that he's a big and *long* bird, from the tip of his tail to the tip of his beak, fools many a gunner into fluffing out only tail feathers with his shot-charge and letting the bird sail merrily on unscathed even after a second flustered barrel. Big game birds, like the pheasant and the Canada goose, are gay deceivers to the guileless beginner in this respect. Unless forewarned, many misses will result before consistent kills are scored.

Proof of how deceptive may be the apparent flight-speed of large birds in the air may be noted in the case of the low-flying aeroplane. As the ship flies over you, perhaps at no greater height than 150 yards, it looks like a slow-moving and easy object to hit—yet it may be travelling easily at more than twice the speed of the fastest-flying game bird.

As experience ripens, however, the gunner wisely begins

[107]

leading the head of all big birds—particularly the cock pheasant in full flight, half of whose length is nothing more than gorgeous tail feathers, which certainly represent no vital vulnerable area.

With respect to establishing correct lead, or forward allowance, on various flying targets—only *you* will know how much *you* should lead, after experience teaches you. Every man leads differently. Some men's subconscious minds work like chain lightning in perfect coordination with their trigger fingers—consequently their lead on flying game is comparatively short. Other gunners, but no less accurate shots, work more slowly in the eye-to-brain-to-trigger-finger sequence and consequently learn by trial and error to lead their birds a longer distance.

Most good shots who are at all conscious of their movements in aiming and shooting at flying targets will agree that the best way to swing on a moving target is to come from *behind* the target—and then at the instant the muzzle races *past* the target (or shortly after) to let 'er go. In fact, that last racing swing past the target, and the trigger-pull itself, happen in such quick sequence that they seem to occur at very near the same instant. But the correct maneuver is to come from behind—race past—*bang!* Never stop the swing of your gun. Follow through. And if you stand correctly, you will follow through—as we told you in the preceding chapters.

The only paradox the author has ever been guilty of originating, with respect to wingshooting, is as follows:

The greatest initial obstacle to the beginner in becoming a good wing shot in the game field, or a good target shot on the Skeet field, is the fact that he has a gun in his hands.

It is well-known to all of us who have been through the mill, that as soon as the shotgun is placed in the hands of the beginner, in the field, that the game bird immediately begins flushing with noisier violence, flies faster apparently than the beginner has ever seen one fly before, and is much more difficult to point at with any feeling of certainty of being "on" the flying target.

As a beginner, if you are disposed to doubt this—take a stroll through good game cover some sunny autumn afternoon behind a good bird dog—but instead of taking a gun with you, carry only a walking-stick. It's an odds-on gamble that you will find, perhaps to your astonishment, that game birds which formerly scared the wits out of you with the roar and fuss of their rise now seem to take wing with not near as much bewildering commotion. You find your nerves comparatively steady. The bird won't be up and away in a flash. Indeed, you may view the rise with a sort of detached deliberation. You may be able to count five before the bird gets out of fair shotgun range.

Swinging your walking-stick up into gun position, you make mental note of the fact that you could kill the bird possibly five times while it is still within good shooting range. And then—and perhaps not until then—you may sit down to ponder why the trick seems so easy to perform with a harmless walking-stick, yet so difficult to achieve when you are armed with a shotgun.

You don't need to wait for the game season to roll around again to try this experiment. You can try it on the Skeet field, and it's a safe bet your experience will practically parallel the foregoing outline. Indeed, in the case of the beginner at Skeet, I am tempted to recommend at least one initial round armed with nothing more lethal than a walking-stick.

The ease with which you can "kill" your targets repeatedly with the harmless walking-stick might be explained thus:

First of all, the walking-stick is a familiar "weapon." You have been pointing with some kind of a stick ever since you learned to walk. The gun, on the other hand, is a distinctly unfamiliar instrument. The stick is light. The gun

by comparison is heavy. The stick has no "sights" on it—
you point it as casually as you point your arm. The gun, on
the other hand, has a little pin sticking up on the center
of the muzzle, called a sight—which, quite naturally, you
assume is put there for the definite purpose of seriously being made use of—whereas the good field or Skeet shot is seldom (if ever) conscious of paying any attention whatever to
this sight on the end of his shotgun barrel when shooting at
game or Skeet targets.

Further, the walking-stick is a silent weapon, never makes
any noise—while the gun has a loud and seemingly vicious
bang. Also, the walking-stick has no recoil—whereas the gun
sometimes (as far as your unaccustomed shoulder is concerned) seems to kick like the Old Harry, to put it mildly.

All of this is a round-about way of saying—that if you
had a light walking-stick that would throw a charge of shot
at normal shotgun velocity, and without any attendant noise
or recoil, probably you could learn to be a pretty fair Skeet
shot within a week or so from the day you first stepped up
to the firing-line on the Skeet field.

But because the gun does have weight—plus a roaring re-
port—plus a certain amount of bucking recoil—the beginner,
as soon as he steps on to the Skeet field with a gun in his
hands, becomes immediately and wholly *gun*-conscious—
whereas with the walking-stick, he was (oppositely) almost
completely *target*-conscious.

In line with the foregoing, you can readily appreciate why
the author feels he has good grounds for stating that the
young shooter will do best to begin with a gun that is neither
too heavy in weight, nor too sharply noticeable in recoil.
Also, we are more or less convinced that the beginner's interest will best be served by selection of the most naturally-
balanced gun he can lay hands on. For this reason, the conventional side-by-side double gun, say in 20 gauge, and

weighing not more than about 6 to 6½ pounds, is recommended.

Obviously, the first task of the beginner at Skeet shooting is to initiate the formation of a sequence of coordination—and to do this, he should have a gun of good balance and handling quality, also reasonably light in weight and recoil, since it is such qualities in a gun that make it easily and quickly *responsive* to the shooter's will—just as the light walking-stick seemed to respond more readily in his untrained hands.

The beginner at Skeet shooting must acquire coordination—at least he must make a beginning of the development of this correlation of eye-to-brain-to-trigger-finger which is vital to good wingshooting.

However, merely telling the young shooter to acquire coordination is like the doctor telling a sick man to get well. The young shooter might go on for months with heavy, ill-fitting gun—wholly absorbed in *gun*-consciousness rather than *target*-consciousness—and under such circumstances, development of coordination might be (almost surely would be) seriously delayed.

Of course, this matter of avoiding too much gun-consciousness might, on the other hand, easily be misunderstood by the beginner at Skeet, thus resulting in his getting out of hand and becoming a wild performer, without any semblance of consistency in his work. For it is a certainty that the beginner must indulge in a certain amount of *initial* gun-consciousness—to the extent that he will know exactly where his gun is pointed, with relation to the target, at the instant it is fired. In fact, I am not so sure but that the beginner's early method of aiming should be more or less meticulous in its attempted precision—for it is at this stage of his training that the beginner will be cultivating and building up within his own personal mechanism a subconscious "sense" of his gun's alignment with respect to the target.

The line of demarcation is necessarily thin here, varying with the individual—as to just how much the beginner should *watch* his gun—and as to just how much he should avoid paying *too much* attention to his gun. Over-stressing the necessity for clearly noting the gun's alignment at the instant of firing may possibly result in the beginner becoming a pokey, meticulous aimer. Too little insistence, however, in this matter of having the beginner *know* his gun's alignment at the instant of firing, may result equally unfortunately—in that the beginner may be led into a wild and sketchy method of prematurely-attempted snap-shooting. Let the beginner be warned of the mistakes he can make by over-indulgence in either direction and so govern himself accordingly.

In all fairness, however, we must state it as our belief that the amount of vision one devotes to both target and gun probably does vary, not only with the individual, but with the age of the shooter and the quality of his vision. It is unquestionably true that the young keen-eyed shooter has such excellent accommodation in his vision that he can easily keep both gun and target, in their relationship, clearly within his vision on about a 50–50 basis. This is proved almost conclusively, it seems to me, by the fact that young Skeet shooters practically dominate in the winning and holding of titles in important Skeet competition throughout the country.

As the shooter grows older, however, either through defective vision, or because of the lower power of visual accommodation that comes with added years, it is probable that 80 or even 90 per cent of the vision may then advantageously be devoted to the target and its immediate area, with possibly not more than 10 to 20 per cent devoted to the gun. Such enforced re-distribution of visual power (to 80–20, or even

90–10 proportion) is possible to the older shooter with years of gunning experience behind him—because this shooter's hands have received sufficient training to "groove" them to the habit of subconsciously, automatically and accurately doing the bidding of *target*-conscious eyes.

In the matter of training the young Skeet shooter to lead his targets correctly at varying angles, let us abandon the old-fashioned and fallacious method that has been the established rule in the past. Why confuse him by telling him, for instance, to lead this target 3½ feet, that target by only one foot, or to hold 10 inches under on another? There are sixteen shots on the Skeet field. Is the young Skeet shooter supposed to keep a notebook in his pocket (scribbled full of such "pearls of wisdom" as you have thus given him) for ready reference at each firing station? Hardly.

To clear up existing misunderstanding and misinformation on this point, let us more correctly classify lead, or forward allowance, in two separate and distinct divisions, thus:

First, there is the correct *mathematical lead*—which can be stated with exact certainty, so long as flight-speed of the target, velocity of the shot-charge and range-yardage are known values. This *mathematical* lead on the Skeet field is between 3 and 4 feet when the target is "taken" at or near the crossing-point of target flight. And I say "between 3 and 4 feet" because the traps may be set to throw slightly faster (or slower) than the regulation Skeet target; or a target may be speeded up by riding with the wind, or slowed down by bucking the wind; or other slight variables may enter.

Second, there is the lead that the shooter ultimately acquires from experience—which is no more than a variable timing interval—and which holds true only for the shooter's own individual speed of swing and developed sense of timing.

So—let the beginner start right by understanding the requirement for the mathematical lead. And let him apply this lead experimentally—by trial and error—except that we insist that he shall apply it from the fundamentally correct principle of the *Minimove Method.*

The *Minimove Method* enforces correct stance—assures correct follow-through—therefore gives the beginner the only dependable method for applying his trial-and-error lead from the safe background of fairly constant factors. That is, with correct stance and pivotal control assured by the *Minimove* principle—the only variable left in the young shooter's formula is the muzzle-target relationship. The vital variable is thus segregated within narrow limits for more intensive study. The young shooter now has but one standard problem to solve (which he can solve only by patient trial and error) instead of sixteen different problems, in each of which all involved factors are unrelated and uncontrolled variables.

In short, give him the *Minimove Method* and let him find his own "spots." He's the only one who can find them (for him) anyway.

Beautiful pivotal control in taking the station 5 lo-trap target, as demonstrated by Mr. Richard Shaughnessy, of Massachusetts, former National All-Bore Champion.

Still another example of the markedly bent pivot-leg. Both legs are bent here in a half-crouch which gives powerful control over (too-heavy?) gun-weight. Mr. G. C. Parker, of Oklahoma, calling for the lo-trap target at station 3.

Quite high muzzle position on the station 1 outgoer. Too high, except for the keen-visioned shooter who can pick up the target quickly and smash it within 15 to 18 yards, as can Mr. Grant Ilseng, of California, shown here.

Station 1 outgoer as shot by Mr. Richard Shaughnessy, using the 16-gauge gun with which he won the National All-Bore Championship a few years ago.

10

THE WILL TO HIT

THE substance of this chapter touches on the prime fundamental of good wingshooting—that strange quality in the human mental-physical make-up which, for want of a better term, we might call *the will to hit.*

It is more or less a job of dealing with subtle intangibles when we attempt to set down in comprehensible black-and-white any cold-type explanation of this lightning-like co-ordination between mind and muscle that seems to be the secret of outstanding superiority in all sports, from boxing to shooting.

Take the great Negro fighter, Joe Louis, for example. If you put Louis up against any one of those knuckle-busting bopp-registers—I mean one of those wallop-weighing machines you see at county fairs that register how hard a man can hit with his best hand—it is entirely possible that the greatest fighter of his age would not be able to show more actual foot pounds of energy in his punch than most of the better "boiler makers" who club each other in the preliminaries leading up to the main event.

Yet those who have fought Joe Louis unanimously concur in the opinion that the "Brown Bomber" has dynamite packed in each hand. Why? Well, principally, I suspect, because Louis was born with that subconscious principle in his make-up which we call *the will to hit.* In other words, his hitting power is so closely coupled to his subconscious reflexes that he functions entirely independently of any thinking apparatus he may or may not possess. Such a fighter in the ring is never slowed up to the tempo of conscious cerebration. His *will to hit* flashes "There—an opening!" and in that split instant, smack! somebody gets hit.

The *will to hit* is a primordial reflex handed down from our early ancestors. It is in no way connected with the cerebral, or thinking part of the brain. Each of us has it in greater or lesser degree. It is the eye, subconscious mind and hand functioning together in a one-man play—"from Tinker to Evers to Chance."

Every great fighter has this close-coupled reflex which enables him to hit with the speed of a rattler's strike. The *will to hit* clicks faster than the speed of thought, thereby enabling the fighter to deliver the maximum power of his "Sunday punch" at the instant of contact. This is the mighty little thing we call *timing*. All the really great figures in sport have it. Great golfers have it. Great tennis players have it. All great wing shots, trap shots and Skeet shooters have it.

Timing in wingshooting does not refer to total time consumed, but to the *sequence relationship of coordinated action*. You can shoot fast, or you can shoot deliberately; yet either in perfect timing.

Watch any of the top-notch Skeet shooters in action and see how uniform they are in their timing—also how uniform they are in their performance! A great wing shot has no really bad days. You and I may shoot beautifully on one occasion, only to falter rather miserably on another. That's where the natural born wing shot comes in—and there is such a thing (all argument to the contrary notwithstanding) as the natural born shot, natural boxer, golfer, tennis player, or baseball batter.

The keen advantage of having the *will to hit* in Skeet shooting is that, upon all occasions, day in and day out, your timing is practically uniform. In the case of such a Skeet shot, there is never more than the slightest variation from correct lead, or forward allowance. Such finely-balanced co-ordination is apparently as rhythmic in its functioning as the ticking of a well-made time-piece.

Leading a flying target, either feathered or clay, is the simplest problem in the world—on paper. For instance, you know the speed of the flying target. You know its initial velocity; also its remaining velocity at practically any within-bounds range on the Skeet field. In the case of the Skeet target, the speed of the flying saucer is roughly 50 feet per second at mid-point in the field, which is approximately where the good shot "takes" it. You also know the speed of your shot charge. So, by the simple process of arithmetic, you can figure quite readily for yourself that, while the shot travels over average 21-yard Skeet range, say shooting from station 4, the target itself flies varyingly from three to four feet during the same interval.

Thus, it is just as simple as rolling off a log to know for a certainty that all you have to do to approximately center the flying Skeet target with your charge of chilled 9's is to see that your barrel is aimed about 3½ feet ahead of the target (and at a point directly in its path of flight) at the instant the gun is fired. Just as simple as that.

But it so happens, that in shooting, all this is far from as simple as it sounds. Lead, or forward allowance, is the most difficult thing in all wingshooting for the coach to explain; or for the novice to understand and master. It is difficult because no two men ever lead exactly alike—and all because no two men have the same speed of coordination, or the same interval of coordination. This interval of coordination in-cludes the space of time elapsing from the instant the eyes see the target, to the instant the trigger finger touches off the shot.

No two men are made alike—either physically, optically, mentally, or temperamentally. Human combinations vary even more than the well-known Yale locks. Therefore, the amount of lead, or forward allowance, to be correctly given the flying target by the individual shooter must vary slightly in the case of each individual shooter—and the same must be discovered by the individual shooter for himself, and only through personal experience.

The automatic swinger (using the *Minimove Method*) doesn't have to lead his target as much as the man who fails to swing his gun with automatic follow-through. The reason for this is easily understandable: The swinger who follows-through automatically, has his gun moving rapidly past the target during the instant his trigger-finger is doing its stuff. The man who doesn't follow-through automatically, will 'most likely retard the speed of his gun-swing when his trigger-finger begins its function in the shooting cycle—with the result that the target, in this shooter's case, gains back part of the previously established lead—in fact, may even exceed and discount the previously established lead, with the result that the shot-charge flies harmlessly behind the target for a clean miss.

The automatic swinger, with unretarded follow-through, may even lead his targets by a shorter margin of forward allowance. Such a gunner can shoot more nearly *at* his target, which one must grant is a much more natural way to shoot at any target. His effortless and automatic follow-through not only maintains speed of gun-swing in the path of the target (while his trigger-finger is performing its part of the bargain) but the fast-swinging barrel itself may actually impart a certain amount of lateral drift to the shot-charge, which may confer added and "automatic" lead at usual Skeet range.

This *will to hit* is a great quality for the field shot to possess. It gives him that resolute assurance that he can hit anything that gets up—and wherever it gets up, ahead of him, right, left, or behind him. A good shot has this feeling in hunting alone, or with only a spaniel, in good "birdy" grouse cover. It's a warm tingling from heels to ears—that keeps him stepping lightly and surely, like a boxer—yet there is no more feeling of "flusteration" in his tingling, keyed-up mechanism than there is in a block of ice, or in a cat poised for a sure-footed lethal pounce.

On the Skeet field the *will to hit* is an invaluable aid to concentration. Anticipating the target's immediate appearance seems to invoke a magnetic, enveloping power. The target's flash-out from the trap opening is the tell-tale that your opponent has "dropped his guard"—*bang!* and you connect right on the button for a puff of black target smoke. You threw your "Sunday punch"—which happened at the moment to be a load of chilled 9's. You knew it couldn't happen otherwise when you *willed to hit*.

It's a keen, tingling swirl of pleasurable emotion—the very tip-top of the art of wingshooting—this *will to hit*. Maybe it's just as well that the humble and pedantic "lead measurer" will never know the fun he's missed!

11

A ROUND OF SKEET

ALTHOUGH a round of Skeet requires the throwing of twenty-five targets, and the firing of twenty-five cartridges, there are only sixteen separate and distinct shots on the field. The four doubles shot from stations 1, 2, 6 and 7 are only duplicates of the singles targets previously fired at. And of course, the twenty-fifth target in each round of Skeet comes as an *optional* shot at the end of a straight run of twenty-four—or, as more frequently happens, it is an enforced *repeat* shot taken immediately after (and on the same target) the scoring of the first miss.

One of the first things a good Skeet shot does when he arrives at the shooting field—and this applies whether it's a match day, or just a practice day—is to study very carefully the target performance from both trap houses. By all means get into this habit of watching target performance before it comes time for your squad to move up to the firing-line. First of all, observe the direction of the wind. Note what the wind is doing to the targets. If a steady nine o'clock wind is blowing—then you are very likely to get a fast-dropping hi-trap target. Incidentally, what the rifleman terms a nine o'clock wind would be blowing across the field from hi-trap station 1 to lo-trap station 7. This same nine o'clock wind will probably result, also, in a rising target from the lo-trap.

Conversely, if you have a three o'clock wind (that is, a wind blowing from station 7 to station 1) you are going to have a rising hi-trap target—and a corresponding sharp-dipping lo-trap target.

Get into the habit of thinking of these things before your squad comes up on the firing-line to shoot. Don't let your observance of peculiarities in target flight "get" you—that is, don't worry over these peculiarities. To be forewarned is to be forearmed. That's all there is to this preliminary caution to be observant. Nearly all Skeet targets are more or less affected by wind. It's a rare day on the Skeet field when we have ideal, still-air conditions. So—regard peculiarities in target flight as natural probabilities, never anything exceptional or difficult.

This kind of cautious observance is all in line with the *Minimove Method*. After all, the basic theory of the *Minimove Method* is simply to eliminate all negative motion from your body—and all negative thought from your mind —once the target is in the air. Therefore, strict attention to the principle of the *Minimove Method* is almost sure to relieve or remove apprehension due to otherwise unprepared mental angle, as well as unprepared physical angle. So watch where the wind is coming from—also observe whether the wind is puffy, or whether it is a constant factor.

It is on windy days that the fast shot is at his best. Or, perhaps we should put it the other way and say, that it is on windy days that the average slow shot is usually at his maximum disadvantage. The fast shot does better than the slow shot on windy days, usually, because he kills his target before it has lost too much of its velocity. As long as the Skeet target has good remaining velocity, wind can't affect it a great deal. But as soon as the target's velocity drops down—then even a mild breeze can affect the line and character of its flight.

This does not mean—under any circumstances—that you should ever try to exceed your natural timing on a windy day. If you are a fast shot, well and good. But if your eyes are slow in their functioning, and if you are rather deliberate and your reactions are a little less speedy than chain light-

[121]

ning, then by all means do not try to exceed your natural timing.

If you are naturally a rather deliberate shot, and you find on any particular day that target flight is a little less than constant—almost erratic—then a calm preview of probabilities and possibilities should enable you to make use of the theory of the *Minimove Method* to rid your mind of the apprehension which, unless it is removed from your make-up, invariably results in strangulated muscle movement. Having thus previously ironed out physical and mental obstacles, you can shoot in your accustomed deliberation—even be extra cautious in your movements—and you will find you can be as sure-footed as a cat, ready to strike in your own time (and according to your own timing) after the target appears—and quite regardless of the peculiarity of the target's flight due to wind effect.

As to the sixteen shots on the Skeet field—let's see how they line up:

First of all, you have the straight-away overhead outgoer at station 1; then the slightly left-quartering incomer.

Moving to station 2, you have a slightly right-quartering outgoer; then a broadly left-quartering incomer.

At station 3, you have a right-quartering outgoer; and almost a left-crossing target on the incomer.

At station 4, you have what amounts to a right-crossing target from the hi-trap and a left-crossing target from the lo-trap.

Now, as you move around to stations 5, 6 and 7, you have the same shots you have just fired at—and smashed, I hope—only now you take them in reverse order. Therefore, they deserve to be classed as distinct and different shots—in the same sense that a right-quartering target is definitely an opposite target from the left-quartering target, as related to the shooter's reversed technique.

On station 5, you have what amounts to almost a right-crossing hi-trap bird; and then a left-quartering outgoer.

Moving to station 6, here you have a more sharply right-quartering incomer; and a left-quartering outgoer.

And at station 7, instead of exactly the reverse of station 1, you have a right-quartering incomer—and a *low* straight-away outgoer—whereas at station 1 you had an *overhead* straight-away outgoer. Both latter targets are straight-away, yet one comes out overhead, while the other rather simulates the easy close-in rise of the game bird in the field.

At station 8 you have two snap shots. At least, I prefer to regard these as snap shots. Some shooters' eyes are quick enough to see these two targets in time to make swinging shots of them. However, I think in the original scheme of things they were designed to be snap shots. Range is not a factor here at station 8. The fact that you kill the station-8 target at 10 yards, or less, means nothing. The important point is—you have to shoot quick. The station-8 shot is a spectacular shot—just the kind of a shot we occasionally get in dense undergrowth in good grouse, woodcock and quail cover. Range is only relative. Under the same conditions, in the game field, it might just as well be a 30-yard shot taken in the same timing. And of course, station 8 not only gives you the right-quartering snap shot from the hi-trap— but also the left-quartering shot from the lo-trap. Both are excellent practice for the game field, as well as being spectacular shots in a colorful shooting game.

Indeed, I wouldn't be at all surprised if these two shots provided much more than half of the real ballyhoo and come-on that has helped Skeet to capture nation-wide popularity in the last dozen years. Lack of the spectacular is keenly missed in any game. That's why rifle shooting is usually dull to the crowd. Revolver shooting is dull, too— until a man like Ed McGivern steps up and starts clipping aerial targets at the rate of six fast shots from a cylinder-gun, all centered before the target hits the ground. Rifle shooting is also dull—until we see a man like Ad Topperwein smash marbles tossed in the air in this great shot's usual spectacular display of uncanny skill.

Anyway, there are your sixteen shots in Skeet—the only sixteen shots you have to master, because the other nine shots are all duplicates. As a matter of fact, there are only four general classes which embrace these sixteen shots—(1) the straight-away target, (2) the crossing target, (3) the quartering target and (4) the snap shot. All sixteen targets on the Skeet field are variations of these four general classes. So it only remains to see what you are going to do with these sixteen simple wingshooting problems, and how fast you can progress in the acquisition of sufficient skill to take them all-straight-in-a-row.

In this connection, it might be interesting for the reader to note an analysis I made of 742 individual rounds of Skeet, shot by 187 individual gunners, in the 9th Lordship all-bore match in the summer of 1937. At that time I thought it would be interesting to Skeet shooters to know just where most of the missing is done on the Skeet field. The chart reproduced herewith shows a percentage proportion of total misses, for each target, at each station, singles targets as well as doubles.

One of the curious facts revealed on this chart, you will observe, is the apparent wickedness of the station-5 lo-trap outgoer. Note from the bar-chart that the station-5 outgoer was apparently the toughest target on the field for 187 shooters in 742 individual rounds of Skeet. The only logical explanation one can offer for the poor performance on this station-5 outgoer is that, after station 4, the shooter falls victim to a *let-down* in concentration. In other words, he is past the station-4 crossing targets, which he feels is an exceedingly difficult pair of targets—and once past this station 4, it seems to me the principal error is merely a let-down—a sort of subsidence of the shooter's natural caution and concentration.

Note, also, in the bar-chart—how in the doubles shooting

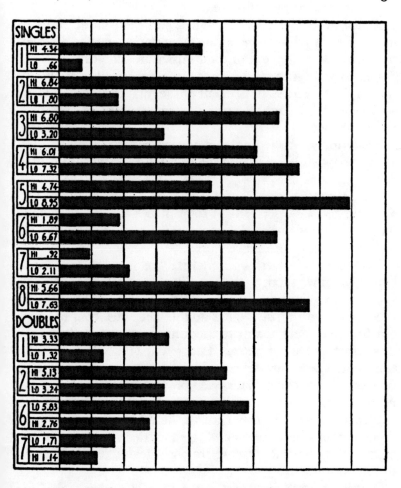

the scoring is slightly better than when the same targets are shot singly:

On station 1, for example, we see a combined percentage

of 5 per cent of total misses on the first two targets in the singles shooting. Yet, when the same targets are shot as a double from the same station 1 a little later, we see only 4.65 per cent of total misses scored.

Again, at station 2, in the singles, 8.64 per cent of the total misses are scored—and yet at the same station, on the doubles pair, only 8.37 per cent of total misses are scored.

On station 6 the tally is very close, practically equal. On the singles targets, 8.56 per cent of the total misses are scored—while on the doubles targets, 8.59 per cent of the total misses are scored.

At station 7, on the singles, 3.03 per cent of the total misses are scored—while on the doubles only 2.85 per cent of total misses are scored.

Summing up, on the eight singles targets from stations 1, 2, 6 and 7, 25.23 per cent of total misses are scored—while on the doubles targets from the same stations, only 24.46 per cent of total misses are scored.

This simply serves to emphasize the fact that we shoot better when we shoot without hesitation—without puttering —without meticulous "riding" of the target. Knowledge of the fact that we must shoot a double keeps us from holding our fire. We come nearer to shooting in our natural timing. Therefore, we shoot better. That's why you have been told time and again throughout this book, never to ride your targets. And of course, steady employment of the *Minimove Method* should also help the shooter avoid this bad habit of riding his targets. In other words, he will be more likely to shoot without hesitation—and to shoot decisively—when his mental and physical "tracks" are both cleared of all obstacles to free movement.

Timing always improves more rapidly under the *Minimove Method*. Apprehension is allayed, or entirely removed —which at one and the same stroke builds confidence. Confidence in turn eliminates indecision—and where indecision no longer exists, we have a shooter who no longer tends to ride his targets, but who shoots in what comes very near being his *natural* timing.

In addition to watching wind direction and target performance before you start to shoot, take in the details of the whole field. Note, if it happens to be a board-walk firing-line, whether loose boards, or broken boards, are to be avoided. Don't let these things surprise you with a "first appearance" just as you arrive at the firing-station. Size up the whole situation in general, so that by the time your squad comes up in turn to shoot, there won't be a shred of apprehension left anywhere in your make-up. Coming on the Skeet field, either for a practice round or for an important match, always handle yourself the same. Treat yourself as though you were a high-strung thoroughbred that requires being led around a little bit to get the feel of the track before the start of the race. Sharpen up your observation for every little thing. The functioning of your powers of observation will also tend to keep your mind off yourself. The mind becomes more keen under such exercise. The power of concentration becomes more virile, more single-purposed.

If considerable wind is blowing, note for instance what effect it has on carrying the shooter's "pull" call to the control house. This can vary according to whether the shooter is upwind or downwind from the control house. Note whether there is any hesitancy on the part of the puller in the control house to release targets at the shooter's call; or whether there is any tendency toward malfunctioning on the part of electrical timer or traps.

Make a habit of exercising your powers of observation. You will find the habit grows quickly—and as it grows it will be good for you and good for your shooting.

Take particular notice of the conditions of the shooting field's background—whether you have a confusing hilltop line for a background, or whether you have a sky background. There are dozens of such little things that the crack Skeet shot never fails to pick up in a few minutes' survey of the field he is about to shoot over. This is one of the things, believe it or not, that helps make him a crack Skeet shot. For just as it is true that most of the misses start from the ground—from the way our feet are positioned—so do not a few misses invariably find their way onto the score sheet because of little things that surprise us, startle us, or that cause us momentary apprehension—in short, triflingly little yet *tremendous* things we should have noticed before we started to shoot.

And keep in mind, always, this thought: *There isn't a hard shot on the Skeet field.*

There is one other point I almost forgot to mention—and it is an important point—*ear protection*. By all means get the habit of putting cotton in your ears on the Skeet field. You may feel it isn't necessary to take this precaution. It is quite possible that the muzzle blast (particularly from the short-barrelled Compensator-equipped 12-gauge gun) won't be painfully or even annoyingly disconcerting to you. But if you spend much time around the Skeet field, week-end after week-end, through five to ten years—then, eventually, you *are* going to notice it.

Or let's put it another way. You won't notice it in your twenties, or possibly not in your early thirties. But after you are forty—then you may wish you had used some sort of ear protection during your twenties and early thirties. The things you do *before* you are forty frequently don't count up on you until *after* you are forty.

To explode a well-known myth—that's all bosh about "life begins at forty." That line was written by a fellow who had passed forty and was whistling to keep his courage up. Also, it was written from the shrewd commercial angle—that its obvious appeal to people past forty would undoubtedly result in the added sale of any book bearing such a title.

In brief, take care of yourself now, so that you won't have to pay later on—and you will in all probability have to pay later on if you don't protect your ears on the Skeet field to-day. It is not pleasant to go through the latter part of your life with ears ringing like sleigh bells. I happen to know—though I can't charge it all to Skeet, since I was so foolhardy as to do much indoor pistol shooting without sufficient ear protection. However, that's neither here nor there as far as I am concerned—but it should be a tip-off to you.

As regards protecting the ears, I have never found anything more effective than cotton. I have tried wool mixed with vaseline, patented ear plugs, even empty .38 Special pistol-cartridge cases. The latter do a fair-enough job; though, of course, the .38 cases are fitted into the ears base-end first. But the most effective of all is cotton.

One of these days, however, I shouldn't be at all surprised to see some smart inventor come along with a pair of "vacuum ear-muffs" which will really deaden the sound and shock (on the ear-drums) of gun-fire.

12

STATION ONE

I N beginning a round of Skeet, bear in mind first of all
that the instructions following are offered from the
viewpoint of the *right*-handed shot. The *left*-handed
shot may oppositely interpret and equally benefit—but for
the purpose of uniformity, the right-handed shot will be
exclusively considered throughout this and succeeding chapters.

Your squad is up and it is your turn to shoot at station 1.
Step up smartly. Your gun is open and empty. Carry your
two shells in your hand if you like—although this might be
considered by some as pressing a bit. Better to start from
scratch from each station—that is, reach in your pocket for
your shells and go through the whole operation of loading
the gun after you reach the firing station—and without preliminaries which might not only do things to you psycho-
logically, but which might also adversely affect nervous
squad mates.

Step up to the firing station smartly and load but one shell
in the chamber—that is, if the N.S.S.A. rule is being strictly
observed on that day. If you are a beginner, it will be best
for you to observe the N.S.S.A. rule of one shell in the gun
anyway, in the singles shooting. But if the rule of the field
permits two shells, then add a shell to the second barrel of
your double gun, or to the magazine of your repeater. For
to load singly, where the rule of the club says two shells
may be loaded—and where shooters are accustomed to having two shells loaded simultaneously—this would undoubt-

Perfect form on the station 1 overhead straightaway—Mr. Alex Kerr, of California, shooting. Left leg is pivot, right leg is pusher, counterbalance and follower.

Station 1—Hi

Station 1—Lo

edly result in irritating delay to your squad mates, waiting for you during the slower process of loading and shooting singly. In short, when in Rome do as the Romans do—but whatever you do, do it safely.

Take your stance in favorable position for the job at hand. Bear in mind that your outgoing station-1 target is to be a straightaway—an overhead straightaway. Take a look at the marker-stake out there at the crossing-point of target flight. That stake is put there to guide you—to give you the line of your target's flight. See that you are in correct position to kill on that line. This is not game shooting. This is Skeet. Take every advantage offered.

Gun movement on this station-1 outgoing target is in the vertical plane only. Therefore, your pivot leg will be the *left* leg—and your pusher, counter-balance and follower will be the *right* leg.

Hold your gun with muzzle inclined upward and pointing at a spot about ten yards out from the hi-trap opening. Your gun movement of course is going to be all *downward* and in the vertical plane. You can't afford any lost or wasted motion here. Some shooters make the mistake of holding their gun at horizontal—then as the target appears the gun muzzle comes up—then instantly changes and starts down in the vertical plane in the path of the target. You can see for yourself what a handicap it is to thus complicate gun movement. Such shooters frequently shoot above (over-shoot) the target because the downward gun movement lacks sufficient momentum due to its late start downward in the vertical plane.

To cut out lost and waste motion is the essence of the *Minimove Method*—the fundamental purpose. So—with your weight shifted out to your left or pivot leg—and with your right leg functioning as counter-balance and follower —and with your gun-muzzle inclined upward and pointing at a spot out about ten yards in front of the hi-trap opening —call for your target.

[131]

You have been told time and again by amateur "experts" that you must aim *so*-many inches under this outgoing target from station 1. Just exactly how you are supposed to know *how*-many inches, nobody ever quite explained to you. Nor shall I attempt an explanation. You do know, however—because I am telling you at this moment—that your shot-load must be directed toward a point *in front of the outgoing station-1 target and in its path*. This means that your gun barrel must point slightly *under* this outgoing target at the instant you fire. We know this is true. Yet when I shoot this target it seems I shoot directly *at* it. Obviously, the downward momentum of my gun automatically takes care of lead, or forward allowance.

I think it's a mistake to tell the beginner to aim a certain number of inches underneath this outgoer target. It has been my observation that if he stops that long to aim, in estimating so-many inches, he invariably stops his gun-swing, too—and shoots *over* in spite of all advice to the contrary.

Strictly speaking, nobody can tell you exactly how to lead any target—and this is where one of the principal advantages of the *Minimove Method* comes in. For if you stand correctly, with properly-pivoted weight and body control, the automatic non-stop momentum of your gun should swing through easily to more or less correct lead. Of course, you won't be able to achieve any particular uniformity in the accuracy of your lead until later. But you will gradually develop a sense of correct timing as experience accumulates. And you'll acquire a sense of timing faster if you'll follow instructions given herein, to kill your targets as often as possible at uniform range—out at crossing-point of target flight.

Mount your gun in strict accordance with advice already given you—that is, keep your eyes on the target and let your hands do the gun-mounting. The hands can do a good job —if you'll let them. As the gun-butt settles into your shoulder

—shoot. Don't ever get into the indecisive rut of "riding" this or any other Skeet target, or of consciously trying to pull a "fine" aim.

Under the downward momentum of your gun, let the muzzle swing under this station-1 outgoer in a quick *approximation*—just make it a good, close guess—and let 'er go. Let off your shot quickly—but never hurriedly. There's a difference. Hasty shooting never taught anyone anything on the Skeet field, or anywhere else. But quick shooting—that is, decisive shooting—this is something else again and quite distinct from the hurried, flustered and usually futile shot.

Make a firm resolution to make each shot count. Develop the will to hit, at least start it. You have to make a beginning sometime, and you can't start any earlier. Determine at the outset that you are going to kill the target you are shooting at or bust a hame-string—and feel really serious about it. After all, you are developing a shooting mechanism. Every shot you fire in dead-earnest is one step forward toward the goal you seek. Every shot you fire carelessly, without sufficient preparation and thought, is not only a wasted shot, but may even set you back half a step.

However, don't let your hard-and-fast resolution—to make each shot count—lead you into the development of the puttering habit. Be as decisive as you can in your gun movement and shooting. Don't hurry—but don't putter.

Now about the incomer at station 1. This is a slightly left-quartering incomer. Therefore, the *left* leg is the pivot leg. The *right* leg is the pusher, counter-balance and follower. A slight swing to the left on the pivot leg is required to kill this target.

Just about 99 out of a hundred gunners make the error here of allowing this station-1 incoming target to "ride" in on them. What they ought to do is to smash this target out not less than 20 yards in front. By so doing, they would

.quicken development of a deadly uniform interval of timing.

The foolish ones on the Skeet field—some of whom are pretty good shots, too—permit this and other incomers to "ride" in on them. By so doing they interrupt and delay the development of a uniform timing interval which they are, or should be, doing their best to crystallize. And thus they go—shuttling back and forth in their progress—trying to develop uniform timing on one kind of shot, then dissipating the advantage gained on this particular shot by firing at the next succeeding target (the incomer) in the slowest possible time. Without realizing it, they violate the first rule of good shotgun shooting by "riding" these incoming targets. Goodness knows what they wait them out for. The nearer such a target travels in toward one, the more difficult it is to hit. Oh, yes it is! What slight advantage is conferred by closer range is more than offset by the fact that the target now requires a *compound* lead. It's not only flying—it's falling. Therefore, it must be led *under* as well as *ahead*. Also, the shot pattern has narrowed at very close range, until it is scarcely wider than the palm of the shooter's hand.

So—by letting such incomers "ride" in within very close range, the shooter is actually piling up errors for himself, one on top of the other—first, by reversing his method and interfering with whatever tendency toward uniformity might already be established in his timing formula—second, by the necessity for allowing for compound lead *under* the target as well as *ahead* of it—and third, by having his shot pattern greatly narrowed in diameter, so that it is more difficult to hit with.

Do not under any circumstances permit any incomer to "ride" in on you at any station on the Skeet field. It is not for nothing that these incomers are called "sucker" shots—for quite without his knowing it, such shots definitely tend to make a "sucker" out of the shooter who is tempted and influenced to change his timing interval completely in "taking" them.

Another reason why these lazy, floating incomers are referred to as "sucker" shots is the fact that they seem to hypnotize the unwary shooter into "riding" them out—until he has practically reached the extreme limit of free-moving gun-swing—at which point he is likely to stop his gun dead and shoot behind. He is quite likely to shoot behind anyhow, because in following a target that is rapidly losing speed, the tendency of the gunner is to reduce the speed of his gun-swing—to the point where his gun will almost "stop on a dime" due to the least hesitation on the part of the shooter, such as may result from the mere decision to pull the trigger.

In summary—pivot your weight out on the left foot and counter-balance with the right foot in taking the station-1 outgoer. Start with gun-muzzle high and chop downward deliberately on the target in a one-movement gun-swing naturally induced by correct stance and also aided by gravity. Shoot in good timing, before the target travels much beyond the 21-yard point in its flight, which is the crossing-point of target flight.

On the station-1 incomer—change your stance slightly before calling for the target, so that your gun is pointing nearer to the lo-trap opening. Pivot your weight on your left leg—and here use your right foot slightly as pusher, counter-balance and follower—because here you have a slightly left-quartering incomer. Don't let the target "ride" in on you. Kill it before it comes much closer than the standard and uniform 21-yard range which your Skeet-shooting mechanism is to become accustomed to.

Here's another thing to remember at station 1: On this incomer—and on other incomers at stations 2, 6 and 7—wait until you see the target smashed before you turn away from your firing station. There's an old saying in archery that can very well apply here, too: *Never turn away from your target until the arrow strikes.* However, if you kill these incomers out where they should be killed, you won't catch yourself leaning toward the tendency here to turn away before completing the shot.

Now let's move to station 2.

13

STATION TWO

H ERE at station 2, you are immediately faced with the prospect of shooting at a target which many shooters dread. Many feel that this station-2 outgoer is the hardest shot on the Skeet field. Of course, the surest way of putting yourself at a decided disadvantage is to fear the target you are about to shoot at—and that's the trouble with a good many shooters of fair-to-intermediate skill on this station-2 outgoer—they fear it, yet don't realize *why* they fear it. But I'll tell you why:

The average right-handed shot who gets up at station 2 to shoot at this right-quartering outgoer makes little or no preparation whatever to correct his pivotal adjustment before calling for the target. Invariably he leans his weight on his left foot—and keeps his weight more or less leaned out on his left foot while he attempts to swing to the right *against* muscular pull! What happens? You have only to try it yourself to know exactly what happens. Where the shooter attempts to swing to the right—yet with weight mostly pivoted out on his *left* leg—here the natural tendency of his gunmuzzle is to travel *upward* on a slightly-inclined plane. Try it and prove it to yourself.

See what a handicap the average shooter thus places on himself, by attempting to shoot in ignorance of the fundamentals which are automatically accounted for in the *Minimove Method*. The station-2 outgoer is invariably missed by over-shooting. Actually, this simple quartering shot ought to be one of the least difficult on the Skeet field. Yet you have seen—on the bar-chart analysis of missed targets—where nearly 7 per cent of all "goose eggs" on the Skeet field are "laid" on this particular target.

Go after this target correctly and most of the difficulties attendant with shooting at it disappear into thin air. Only correct stance and correct pivotal distribution of weight, as already outlined in the *Minimove Method,* will eventually eradicate the fear that the average Skeet shooter feels at the prospect of shooting at this station-2 outgoer.

Stand correctly and the station-2 outgoer is practically as easy as any target on the Skeet field to smash. Stand with your weight shifted to the *right* leg. The pivot leg on this shot is the *right* leg. The pusher, counter-balance and follower leg is the *left* leg. The best way for the average shooter to stand, I should advise, is to slightly "break" the left leg at the knee—to remind it in advance of its duty as pusher, counter-balance and follower. This is an important point for the average shooter to learn. The good golfer already knows this trick of weight shift—will have had to learn it, in fact, to become a good golfer.

With your weight pivoted on the *right* leg—and with the *left* leg slightly crooked, or "broken," to begin its function as pusher, counter-balance and follower—we are all set to call for the station-2 outgoer. As the target appears, and as your gun comes to shoulder, notice how smooth is your swing. Note particularly how easy it is to keep the swing of your gun in the plane of target flight, whereas previously it seemed difficult or almost impossible for you to keep from swinging in a slightly rising plane, which all too frequently resulted in just another over-shot "goose-egg" on your score-sheet.

That's all there is to this station-2 outgoer—nothing more. So let's turn our attention to the station-2 left-quartering in-comer:

[138]

Station 2—Hi

Station 2—Lo

Station 3—Hi

Station 3—Lo

Station 4—Right

Station 4—Left

Station 5—Hi

Station 5—Lo

On the station-2 incomer—now shift your weight to the left leg. This is a left-quartering target. Therefore, the pivotal leg is the *left* leg on this shot. The *right* leg assumes the role of pusher, counter-balance and follower. Change your position slightly—so that when you call for the target your gun-muzzle will be pointing over fairly close to the opening in the lo-trap, where the station-2 incomer is about to come out. You are going to smash this target at the height of your swing at the crossing-point of target flight, 21 yards out or thereabouts.

And now again—don't let this target "ride" in on you. I know it's a temptation to do so. But don't permit any target on the Skeet field to change your interval of timing. Keep hitting your targets at one point as uniformly as you possibly can. You can't do this in the doubles, of course. But on most of the other shots you can keep your timing interval adjusted to close uniformity. The ideal "killing area" is the five yards in the center of the field—2½ yards to either side of the crossing-point of target flight. Never permit an incomer to "ride" in to you beyond this "killing area." To do so will involve a confusing change in your timing interval.

This is one of the most important points in Skeet—to stick to your uniform interval of timing as closely as possible. Don't permit yourself to "ride" any target, particularly not the easy incomer, which most beguilingly invites one to dwell on it—to his subsequent confusion.

That's all there is to station 2—and of course when it comes to the double at this station, simply adjust your stance at an intermediate position so that you will kill the outgoer at the crossing-point of target flight and kill the incomer about 8 to 10 yards nearer the gun.

Before concluding, here is an interesting thought in connection with gun position that, while it will be mentioned only here, applies practically all the way around the Skeet field, from station 1 to station 8:

This has to do with how you hold your gun, whether the muzzle is held more or less horizontal, or held high. Personally, I like to carry my gun-barrel at a very slight upward angle with the horizontal. I like to bring my gun *up* on a target, rather than *down* on a target from the highly-held muzzle position. On the hi-trap outgoer at station 2, for example, I hold the gun-muzzle just underneath the line of target flight and out from the trap opening about 5 to 7 yards.

Some shooters hold their gun-muzzles closer to the trap opening. They have eyes that see the target quicker than mine do. The trick is to start after the target as soon as you can see it. I don't believe it is possible for the human eye to see the target clearly much before it has travelled about 3 to 4 yards out of the trap. Some eyes are slow, some are rapid in picking up the target.

I prefer to keep my gun-muzzle slightly *underneath* the line of target flight, and to bring it *up* on the target. It is my theory that the gunner should be definitely target conscious—and that he should never see much of his gun until just an instant or so before letting off the shot. After all, one should give his trained hands an opportunity to "do their stuff." They do a good job where one has the confidence to trust them. It also seems to me that one can be more accurate in bringing the gun *up*—against the steadying resistance of gravity—than by bringing it down on a target.

In this connection, I recall the answer given by a well-known pistol shot here in the East who was asked one time whether he brought his sights *up* on the bull's-eye, or *down*. "Well," he replied, "when my gun is above the bull, I bring it *down* and shoot—and when it's below the bull, I bring it *up* and shoot."

That's what we might do in the field. But I still prefer to "come up on the bull"—and when I'm forewarned of the shot I also like to carry my shotgun below the line of vision and come up on the target. And you do as *you* like. I suppose the right way here lies mostly in how one feels about it—for the way one feels can conceivably be a reflection of some inner urge which perhaps thoroughly justifies the method.

I believe, however, that shooters who use light-to-medium gun-weight, particularly those who have had considerable shooting experience, handle their guns on the Skeet field as I handle mine—that is, with barrel only slightly inclined upward and held slightly beneath the line of target flight while calling for the target.

I have observed, also, that shooters using *heavy* guns quite commonly employ the high muzzle position—and there would seem to be some sound reason for their doing so—for with the muzzle of the heavy gun held high, gravity thus assists them in overcoming the inertia of gun-weight in starting initial movement of the gun in the path of the flying target.

So let's get on to station 3.

14

STATION THREE

THE station-3 quartering outgoer causes a good bit of missing—not because it is a difficult target, for it isn't—but because the shooter is apt to let down in his caution and concentration over having just passed the more difficult station-2 outgoer. With the station-2 outgoer behind him, hit or missed, our shooter breathes a sigh of relief and perhaps prepares to sort of take it easy for a while. Then all of a sudden, *bango!* and before you can say Jack Robinson he has missed the station-3 outgoer as well. This same let-down in natural caution and concentration plays havoc on another station farther on, which we will tell you about when we get to it.

For the present, the problem is just as simple as rolling off a log. On the station-2 outgoer, here again the pivot leg is the *right* leg. Shift the weight in greater or lesser degree to the right leg and "break" the *left* leg to prepare it in advance to follow out its function as pusher, counter-balance and follower. Calling for the target from this position, note with what ease and absolute freedom from mental apprehension you start your gun-muzzle from behind and race after the target. Your gun-swing is as smooth and unretarded as a roulette wheel whirling on its groove of steel ball bearings. Your left leg readily yields and follows with the turn of your body, and the momentum of swinging gun-weight goes through as smooth and slick as a whistle. Also, you won't find your gun-muzzle swinging upward in an inclined plane in spite of all you can do to try and hold it down in the path of the target's flight.

Turning your attention now to the station-3 incomer, here again comes the weight-shift. On this target, the pivot leg is the *left* leg—and the *right* leg should be "broken" slightly at the knee to prepare it for its assisting function as pusher, counter-balance and follower. And here again, on this station-3 incomer, don't let the target "ride" past the crossing-point of target flight. You can change your stance slightly so that as you are ready to call for your target your gun-muzzle will be pointing over very close to the lo-trap opening. Then, when you call, and when the target snaps out—go after it smoothly, swinging on the pivot of your left leg and maintaining the steadiness of your swing and balance with the assistance of the right leg—and smash that target cleanly at or near the crossing-point of target flight. Above all, don't "ride" it.

Take the same advice here as has been given you on previous stations—never let the target "ride" past the point where you have had ample time to kill it. Kill this easy incoming target in the same uniform timing you have employed before—which you are seeking, through constant practice, to thoroughly ingrain into your shooting mechanism.

That's all there is to station 3. Pivot on the right leg and follow with the left on the outgoer—then pivot on the left leg and follow with the right on the incomer—and don't waste any time killing either of them. Both should be smashed cleanly within an approximate 5-yard space in the center of the field, two to three yards either side of the crossing-point of target flight.

Now let's get on to station 4.

15

STATION FOUR

THE two targets at station 4—the right-crossing hi-trap target and the left-crossing lo-trap target—account, on the average, for more than 13 per cent of all targets missed on the Skeet field. That's a high percentage, much higher than it ought to be. The only reason I have to offer, to explain the undue amount of missing that takes place here at station 4, is the fact that the shooter invariably takes too much time in killing a crossing target. The shooter takes too much time because he sees the target coming across his line of vision in its long, sweeping flight. On an outgoing quartering target, he sees the target speeding away from him —getting out of range—and he goes after it faster. But on the two crossing targets at station 4—well, they look so easy. The tricky part of it is—when you let a Skeet target fly very far past the crossing-point of target flight, that target has lost much of its velocity and is beginning to drop rapidly. Also, if any considerable amount of breeze is blowing, that target may begin doing tricks. It may drop faster than you expect it to. Or you may be expecting it to drop, yet instead of dropping, it may sail serenely on the level, or even rise slightly. Wind does things to targets where the target's remaining velocity is low.

The average shooter has a deplorable habit of "riding" both of these easy crossing targets. And because he "rides" them, he overshoots fast-dropping targets which have flown thirty yards before he pulls trigger—or he falls into that other error, that invariably results from "riding" any target, which is missing by shooting behind.

Also, of course, the error of shooting behind is always aided and abetted by improper stance, improper weight-shift and poor muscular control.

The station-4 hi-trap crossing target is a right-swinging shot—therefore, the *right* leg is the pivot leg—and the *left* leg acts as pusher, counter-balance and follower.

Conversely, the station-4 lo-trap crossing target is a left-swinging shot—therefore, the pivot leg in this case is the *left* leg—while the *right* leg functions as pusher, counter-balance and follower.

So you see, it is just a case of the simple old *Minimove Method* following you right around the Skeet field—and if you follow *it* around the Skeet field, you should be agreeably surprised and delighted in a very short while at the upward turn in your scoring skill. To be sure, it will take you some time to accustom yourself to the trick. At first, you will be thinking too much of it and this will distract your attention away from the target. But as you practice the simple movements of the *Minimove Method,* not only in shooting on the Skeet field, but in dry-shooting practice, it will rapidly become a more or less fixed part of your subconscious shooting mechanism.

There is nothing to add—no further advice necessary—beyond pivoting your weight on the *right* leg and slightly 'breaking" the *left* leg to act as pusher, counter-balance and follower, when calling for the hi-trap station-4 target. And contrariwise, shift your weight to the *left* leg and slightly "break" your *right* leg ready to assume its duties as pusher, counter-balance and follower, when calling for the lo-trap station-4 target.

Don't "ride" either target at station 4. Break both in the same uniform timing you are seeking to make a fixed part of your shooting mechanism. Try, try—everlastingly try—to stamp this uniform timing interval indelibly into your make-up.

Now let's move on to station 5.

16

STATION FIVE

ELL, here we are at station 5—so watch your step. Station 5 allegedly has a horseshoe in its glove! —somewhat reminiscent of station 3, only more so. According to my previously mentioned analysis of 742 individual rounds of match Skeet shot by 187 shooters, the station-5 targets account for nearly 14 per cent of all the "goose eggs" scored on the Skeet field. The easy hi-trap incomer, of all things, accounts for nearly 5 per cent of the total number of misses on the Skeet field. And the station-5 lo-trap outgoer—well, according to the figures, here's where you meet the toughest shot on the Skeet field.

Now don't get the idea from the foregoing that the station-5 outgoer actually is tough. The difficulty here is mostly psychological. That's the only logical way to account for the fact that this single target—the station-5 lo-trap outgoer—accounts for nearly 9 per cent of the total misses scored at Skeet. Such an easy target has no business throwing otherwise good shots into such confusion.

The station-5 outgoer bugaboo is purely psychological, as has been said—only it happens to be one of the most dangerous psychological bugaboos, because it seems to wear naught but a benign smile—just like the cat that ate the canary. In other words, having more or less successfully passed the two station-4 crossing targets—which many shooters miss—and which many more shooters fear—the shooter is lulled into a state of restful repose on coming up to station 5. This is one of those easy intermediate stations, says he, one of the soft spots. The two station-4 "cut-throats" are in the background. The No. 6 outgoer is too far ahead to worry about. So you are going to take these two station-5 targets right in your stride—just like that. So you up and in all probability smash the easy station-5 incomer. Aha, you are further assured—and your feeling of restful calm becomes even more restful and more calm—and then, *bango!* it happens. That station-5 outgoer, which looked as big as a pie-plate—as easy to hit as a bull with a bass-fiddle—has escaped from your pattern as neat and slick as a whistle!

That's all, in my opinion, there is to the sad story behind this station-5 outgoer. Shooters simply arrive at a let-down in natural caution and concentration. And in that moment of let-down they will miss this target—which can be tricky, but which is never as tricky as the analysis of misses indicates.

On the right-quartering hi-trap incomer at station 5—this of course is a right-swinging shot. The pivot leg is the *right* leg. The pusher, counter-balance and follower leg is the *left* leg. Stand in position so that you can smash this target right out at the crossing-point of target flight.

Stand with your weight pivoted on the right leg—and with your left knee slightly "broken" and ready for its function as pusher, counter-balance and follower. Call for your target —and break that target in the same uniform interval of timing that I have been drilling you on for lo, these many pages. Don't let this incomer "ride" in to you. Don't hurry your shot, of course. But don't delay it either. Kill this target quickly, decisively—and let the referee call it and the scorer mark it up to your credit without further ado.

Now turn your attention to the station-5 left-quartering outgoer from the lo-trap. This is a left-flying target—hence the weight must be shifted to the left leg. The *left* leg is

[148]

the pivot leg. The *right* leg functions as pusher, counter-balance and follower.

Take your stance for the station-5 outgoer and stand in shooting position to smash the target at crossing-point of target flight. Your weight is pivoted on the *left* leg. Your *right* leg is slightly "broken" at the knee to start its function as pusher, counter-balance and follower. Now call for the target—and again, don't "ride" it. You should find this target pie-easy—or, at least, that its difficulty has been generally over-rated.

Now let's go on to station 6.

17

STATION SIX

~~~~~~

THE two station-6 targets represent, approximately, the station-2 targets reversed. My analysis showed that the station-2 singles targets account on the average for 8.64 per cent of total misses; while the station-6 singles targets account for 8.56 per cent of total misses.

The only reason why the station-6 singles show a slight percentage reduction of misses is the fact that about 92 per cent of all shooters are right-handed—and the right-handed shot seems to prefer swinging to the left, as he does on the station-6 outgoer—rather than swinging to the right, as he is forced to do on the station-2 outgoer.

I have always thought that this preference, as to direction of swing, was slightly mixed up, perhaps even groundless. I myself am a right-handed shot, yet prefer to swing to the right. One of my good friends has raised the question as to whether this preference of mine might not be due to long years of hunting in the field, where I always try, whenever possible, to be on the right of my hunting partner, and of course take birds flying out to the right.

However, I doubt whether this is entirely the reason why I prefer the right-crossing target, even though a right-handed shot. On the right-crossing target, swinging to the right, my face is pressed into the comb of my gun stock. Whereas, on the left-crossing shot, swinging to the left, I feel I sometimes make the mistake of "leading with my face" and unconsciously pull my cheek out of contact with the comb—

Station 6—Hi

Station 6—Lo

Station 7—Hi

Station 7—Lo

a fault that is almost sure to result in missing behind—or at least hitting poorly with only the front fringe of the pattern. Beyond this, I am not sure I can properly account for this non-average preference of mine for the right-crossing shot—while most other right-handed shooters definitely prefer the left-crossing shot and swinging to the left.

I do know, however, that swinging either to the right, or to the left, should make not the slightest difference to the shooter so long as he makes use of the principle of the *Minimove Method*. As already pointed out, in discussing the station-2 outgoer, I truly believe that the average right-handed shot finds the right-quartering or right-crossing target difficult only because he tries to go after it from the definitely wrong stance of trying to employ his left leg as pivot.

Where the right-handed gunner resorts correctly to the use of the *right* leg as pivot-leg on the right-quartering or right-crossing shot, here his gun-muzzle just naturally flows into the path of the target with smooth and effortless acceleration. In the same way, on the left-quartering or left-crossing target, if he correctly uses his *left* leg as pivot leg (which he is naturally inclined to do anyhow, being a right-handed shot) then he will have no difficulty whatever on this kind of shot. His "follow-through" is sure to be smooth, effortless, speedy—and accurate.

The station-6 incomer is another "sucker" shot. A sucker shot, in my estimation, is not so-named because just any sucker can hit it—but because such a shot influences a shooter to *become* a sucker if he interrupts his uniformity of timing in order to "ride" such a target into abnormally close range.

The time to kill this target is when it has reached the crossing-point of target flight—out at about 21-yard range.

The station-6 incomer is a right-quartering incomer. Therefore, the *right* leg is the pivot leg—and the *left* leg, slightly "broken" at the knee to prepare it for its correct function as pusher, counter-balance and follower, takes the supporting role.

Call for the target. When it makes its appearance and about the time it reaches the 21-yard point in its flight—smash it. Don't dally with it. Don't "ride" it. Smash it in your standard and uniform interval of timing. Never make an exception to this rule.

On the station-6 outgoer—here you have the mild and easily-solved problem of the left-quartering outgoer. Therefore, the *left* leg is the pivot leg—and the *right* leg, slightly "broken" at the knee to suggest to it in advance its function as pusher, counter-balance and follower, takes the supporting role.

Shooting this station-6 outgoing target according to the basic fundamental of the *Minimove Method* your gun-swing starts smoothly and effortlessly—and your shot-load overtakes and envelopes the target like the curling lash of an expert's bullwhip. You can scarcely miss if you function according to natural principles—if you're any kind of shot at all.

And now on to station 7 for a couple of very *restful* shots —yet beware!

18

STATION SEVEN

THESE two station-7 shots are the easiest pair on the Skeet field. On the singles they account for only 3.03 per cent of the total number of misses on the Skeet field. On the doubles, however, the boys all do better on this pair—simply because they shoot 'em faster. The doubles at station 7 account for only 2.85 per cent of total misses—which should provide a cue for you!

If ever there was a target which was beguiling to the shooter in its "plaintive" entreaty to let it "ride" in on him, this hi-trap incomer at station 7 is that target. Do you know what sometimes happens when the shooter permits this sucker shot to "ride" in on him? It's the old mistake—well-known to expert archers, and to some who are not so expert —of actually starting to turn away while the shot is being fired. I have already mentioned elsewhere in this book this archery rule—never to turn away from your target until the arrow strikes. It's a good rule.

But if you shoot this station-7 singles incomer in your established uniform interval of timing—and smash it out 21 yards at the crossing-point of target flight—you will never miss this target by turning away from it before completing your shot. Smack it where it should be smacked—out at the crossing-point of target flight!

This hi-trap incomer at station 7 is a slightly right-quartering incomer. Therefore, the *right* leg is the pivot leg —and the *left* leg again assumes its function as pusher, counter-balance and follower. Don't neglect this pivotal weight-shift at any station on the Skeet field—however easy the target may appear. Be sure that you are in correct *pivotal* position with the one leg—and in correctly relaxed condition with the opposite leg—before calling for your target. Smashing the target will then be smooth, sure and effortless —and your timing should be uniform.

Don't neglect or overlook this tremendously vital detail before calling for each and every target on the Skeet field.

Now we come to the lo-trap outgoer at station 7. This is a straight-away. Therefore, the motion of the gun is in the vertical plane entirely. Therefore, also, weight should be pivoted lightly on the *left* foot—with the *right* foot assuming its corresponding function as counter-balance and follower. No need for any "pusher" service on this rising, straight-away shot. Just steady support—and balance.

You have (undoubtedly, by this time) been told variously to aim high on this target—also, possibly, to aim low—and perhaps one or two friendly shooters have even advised you to aim straight at this target.

All three bits of advice are more or less correct "according to their lights." But if you shoot this target in the uniform timing interval already urged on you (in foregoing chapters) you will hold on this target just so that your gun-muzzle touches the bottom edge of the target. I don't mean, of course, to aim with any such puttering precision as that might sound like—but simply shoot *at* it.

Where the gunner shoots this target at 10-yard range, or less, here it's a rising target and the gunner must needs "blot it out" before pulling the trigger. But where you shoot the target as I have already advised, at about the 21-yard point in its flight, then shoot at it—have the target "sitting" just on top of your gun muzzle.

For the slow shot who fiddles and dallies with his target until it "rides" out to 30 yards—here the target begins the definite downward curve in its trajectory and of course must be shot "under" to be hit squarely.

But it should be unnecessary for you to remember any such monkey business as holding over, or under, this target. For if you shoot in the correct timing interval—and the principle of the *Minimove Method* encourages the development of this correct timing interval—then you can hold in the most natural style of all on this station-7 outgoer and shoot directly *at* it.

Now let's get on to station 8—where there's real work to be done.

19

STATION EIGHT

T HE two station-8 targets are the really spectacular shots of the Skeet field. Some people don't like them. This, I suspect, is primarily because they don't properly understand these station-8 shots, in their relationship to field shooting. They somehow fail to perceive that these two shots have a definite place in the repertoire of the finished wing shot.

As far as color and interest are concerned, I am just as certain as I am of the fact that I am setting these words down here, that the two station-8 shots are responsible in no small way for the present-day wide-spread popularity of Skeet. For it was these two station-8 shots on the Skeet field of more than a decade ago that gave the innocent bystander the psychological "jab in the arm" that resulted in him, too, becoming a Skeet enthusiast.

Some stand-offish old game shots (most estimable fellows, too) openly criticized the station-8 shots because of the short range at which both of these targets are smashed. It has been suggested, rather unkindly perhaps, that this viewpoint seems devoid of any of the imaginative quality that ought to go hand-in-hand with the art of wingshooting. Personally, I think such criticism of the station-8 shots simply represents misunderstanding. After all, range is only relative with reference to these two shots on the Skeet field. It makes no difference whatever, it seems to me, whether you smash a target at 8 yards, or at 28 yards, so long as your timing mechanism is forced to function at top speed—and this is exactly what the station-8 targets do accomplish—forcing the gunner to shoot in the same fast timing he would employ in thick grouse cover, or in good woodcock and quail cover. At any rate, he would have to employ this fast station-8 timing if he brought many birds to bag in the heavy cover where one usually finds much of his best shooting.

The station-8 shots are neither of them one whit different from snap shooting in thick game cover—except for the irrelevant fact that the station-8 targets are usually killed within 10 yards, frequently within 6 to 8 yards by the slower shot. But the range differential is relative and in a sense only arbitrary, while the timing and the demand made upon the gunner's shooting mechanism is identical. Of course, the clay target hit with fifty pellets at 10-yard range is much more spectacular than a clay target hit with, say, five pellets at 35-yard range. In which respect, as has already been mentioned, the station-8 shots on the Skeet field have furnished much of the real dramatization of a new shotgun game—have no doubt supplied much of the come-on that has brought Skeet up to its present high level of popularity.

Unfortunately, I feel, the British deleted the station-8 targets from their version of the American game of Skeet. Perhaps "ignored" is a better word. For what reasons our Anglo-Saxon cousins chastise themselves with total abstinence from certain obviously pleasurable pursuits, this I cannot answer. They don't even use decoys or callers, either artificial or live, in their duck shooting.

Probably the reason they don't use the station-8 shots in Skeet is that they do relatively little of our American style of so-called "rough" shooting. Much of the British gunner's game is driven over him by paid beaters. Thus, not anywhere near as frequently does an occasion present itself where the game may be seen for only a split-second time interval, such as is quite commonly the case in our American "rough" (as well as ruffed) grouse shooting. The British sportsman quite naturally feels that our American station-8 shots on the Skeet field are wholly impractical as far as his game shooting is concerned. Indeed, the average British gunner has not yet arrived at the point where he considers Skeet anything but a practice game for his field shooting—while over here in America (and by America I include Canada to the north and Mexico to the south) Skeet has developed far beyond its earlier status as "a gun game for the game gun." In fact, Skeet is definitely a game in its own right and "played" as such by some thousands of registered tournament shooters.

There has always been a dither of argument, pro and con, as to whether the station-8 targets should be considered as definitely snap shots—or whether they are more or less the same kind of shots encountered on the other stations of the Skeet field—in that it might be possible to swing on them in the same general method, though in faster timing. The secret —and the settlement—of this momentous argument is that the difference between the station-8 targets and all other targets on the Skeet field lies not so much in the targets themselves, as in the shooter's capabilities in meeting the demands of the two station-8 targets.

In other words, there are shooters who can swing and lead on these targets by employing the same method they use on other stations on the Skeet field—only, of course, the timing mechanism is greatly speeded up at station 8. Shooters who can perform thus, in the usual swinging style, on the station-8 targets, are invariably those whose vision is excellent—therefore, they are not forced to focus their eyes on the targets alone and depend on well-trained hands to take care of manipulation of the gun—but simply have sufficient visual power to see clearly both the target and gun in correct relationship during the mounting and swing. To these fortunate possessors of exceptional vision, therefore, the station-8 targets vary but little (except in the matter of

[158]

Station 8—Hi

Station 8—Hi

Station 8—Lo

Station 8—Lo

speeded-up timing) from targets shot at all other stations around the Skeet field.

The shooter who can take the station-8 targets in swinging style can make use of the same average placement of his feet that he uses on the other Skeet stations. But the shooter who must use the snap style here at station 8—this shooter must spread his feet a littler farther apart to give maximum leverage control for fast gun-movement—because he sees the target only after it has travelled farther toward him, hence must mount his gun and fire within a shorter time limit.

The author, due to visual limitations as well as natural preference, always takes these station-8 targets as true snap shots. We believe that the man who fails to take them so fails to enjoy some of the extra color of the Skeet game—and also fails to quite round out his wingshooting practice. For the snap shot has a definite place in field shooting. However, every man to his own poison—and if taking the station-8 targets one way, or the other, results in higher *scoring* percentage, why, obviously, this is the way for the shooter to handle these two shots at station 8.

As far as we personally are concerned, both station-8 shots must be taken in true snap style—seeing only the target and trusting implicitly to the years of training that have gone into our hands, and trusting the hands to obey absolutely the dictate of the eyes and to point the gun where it should be pointed to smash the target. My good friend, Mr. Harry L. Betten, well-known Pacific Coast wildfowler and outdoors writer, in a letter some years back, coined a beautifully descriptive phrase for this style of shooting—he calls it *shooting with the eye of faith.*

Before we thoroughly understood our present reaction to these station-8 targets—and also before we properly sensed the true relationship of the man with first-class visual accommodation to these same targets—we frequently used to advise that the correct way to shoot at station 8 was to "feel" for the

[159]

target. At any rate, that's the closest we could come to describing our personal reaction to it. In short, we see the target—dare not trust to delayed visual accommodation to see
the gun also—but "feel" for the target in what amounts to
pure snap-shooting style, seeing the target clearly, but paying
no conscious attention whatever to the gun.

In wingshooting, however—which is always a highly in-
dividualistic function and performance anyhow—there is
always the danger of slightly misinterpreting to others—even
when one knows what he himself does. It comes as a great
revelation occasionally, to learn wherein one's capabilities
and methods actually differ from the capabilities and methods of other shooters. But after enough years of study of the
subject, eventually we come to the point where we are will-
ing to approach the subject humbly and with a sincere hope
that we may not inadvertently employ the language of confusion. It is in line with this feeling that we have thus dwelt
on the two separate methods of shooting the two station-8
targets on the Skeet field. For there are two methods, no
doubt of that—and the swinger, with good vision, who sees
the target quickly—and the snap shot, either with or without
good vision—these two must choose, each for himself, how he
himself should best shoot these two targets. And the old
"tell-tale" score-sheet is a pretty good guide.

Of course, whether you shoot these targets in snap style,
or swinging style, has nothing whatever to do with correct
stance—the simple fundamentals of the *Minimove Method*
apply in either case. In line with the *Minimove Method*,
the shooter may place himself so that he will be forced to
make only a minimum of adjustment in his shooting position
after the target appears in the air, and as he begins the rapid
sequence of gun-mounting, leading and firing.

On the hi-trap station-8 target, first of all, determine at
approximately what point in the target's flight your vision
and timing interval will permit you to shoot and hit. To

smash the target after it has flown only 10 to 12 yards requires very fast timing. The average shooter will smash this target only after it has travelled about 15 yards. What we are trying to get at, however, is to establish the line of your individual fire so that you can stand in such position as will reduce subsequent movement to a minimum after the target is in the air. And for the average shooter, I think it best to stand so that the gun rests in the hands with its muzzle pointing toward a spot 10 to 15 feet to the right of the hi-trap house.

The hi-trap station-8 target is, of course, a slightly right-quartering incomer. Therefore, the *right* leg is the pivot leg —and the *left* leg functions as pusher, counter-balance and follower.

In the case of the swinging shooter, who deliberately leads this hi-trap station-8 target, the feet can be placed rather more closely together and weight distribution is very nearly equal, though of course slightly shifted more to the right pivot leg.

With the snap shot, the feet are placed slightly wider apart to give greater leverage control—but from here on it is the same—weight distribution must be almost equal, though slightly more on the right pivot leg, and the muscles in both legs should be maintained at "live tension" similar to the stance employed by the boxer poised to throw his Sunday punch.

At the appearance of the target, the gun should come upward from *below*. This station-8 hi-trap target is a rising (as well as quartering) target with relation to the shooter. Therefore, the gun's movement in the vertical plane should be in one direction only—*upward*. This is a vital point to observe—because one so frequently sees poor performers on the skeet field start from the high gun position here—then at the appearance of the target, down go their muzzles underneath —then try to come upward again. They score frequent misses simply because the downward momentum of the gun is too much to overcome in the short time interval. Their subsequent upward movement of the gun-muzzle, trying desperately to catch up with the target, too often scores a miss by throwing the shot-load at least a foot behind the on-speeding target.

So make sure that the gun-muzzle starts from slightly below the level of the trap-house opening—and then, in one direction only (upward) goes into high gear from initial movement, to race and catch up with the target with the shot-load.

Summarizing: On the hi-trap station-8 target—pivot on the *right* leg—push with the *left* leg—keep both legs tensed for powerful leverage—start with your gun-muzzle just underneath the trap opening and swing on the target in one direction only, until you catch up with, pass and smash it into black smoke with the shot-load.

On the station-8 lo-trap target—here the situation is reversed. Here the *left* leg serves as pivot leg—and the *right* leg functions as pusher, counter-balance and follower.

Facing the station-8 lo-trap target, here again let the gunner carry his gun at a slight outward (left-hand) angle. Stand so that your gun-muzzle points toward just about where you will first catch sight of this lo-trap target.

Hold your muzzle just under the point where this target appears to your vision. You may catch sight of it 3 or 4 yards out of the trap—or it may travel as much as 5 yards before you see it clearly.

Let me repeat the same warning on this target—never carry the muzzle high. If you do—at the instant the target is sprung, down will come your muzzle—then you will undertake the hopeless struggling effort to get back in time to catch the on-speeding target. Usually you won't make it and will score a miss. When you do make it, it will be more a matter of luck and you will "scratch" the rear of the target with the front fringe of your close-packed pattern.

Call for the target with gun-muzzle just a few inches underneath where you first catch sight of this target—then your gun-muzzle travels "the shortest distance between two points"—in other words, in a straight line from the point where you catch sight of the target to the point where you overtake and smash it.

Your *left* leg acts as pivot leg on this lo-trap station-8 target and your *right* leg acts as pusher and counter-balance. However, the principal function of the *right* leg will be in its "pusher" function. This is a quick shot, needs plenty of leverage power—put everything you've got into it—for it is one of the toughest targets on the Skeet field, by actual analysis, as you have already noted.

In addition to employing the fundamental principle of the *Minimove Method* on station 8—I also have some "medicine" for the beginner, as well as for the experienced shot who momentarily finds himself off form on these two station-8 targets. My method of helping these two classes of shooters may be outlined as follows:

For the beginner—here the "dose" must start mild and increase only as skill (and particularly confidence) increases. The beginner I place back 5 yards out from station 7—that is, in taking the station-8 hi-trap target. Thus, the beginner is standing 35 yards from the hi-trap house. It is no difficult trick for him to hit this incoming target before it passes him at this shooting position. After he has broken two or three targets standing here, then I advance him another 5 yards, at which point he is located 30 yards from the hi-trap. Here the shot will be a little more difficult, but on the breaks he scores he will gradually gain confidence. From here I recommend advancing the beginner only a yard at a time. It may take the whole of an afternoon, or possibly a subsequent afternoon the following week-end, to get up somewhere near station 8. But—if he shows any stubborn inclination to ride his hi-trap target too far—and you suspect that his capability in this direction is not as limited as he imagines—then I recommend suddenly giving him *opposite* treatment.

This opposite treatment at station 8 is a sort of third-degree method. I reserve it almost exclusively for those who pretty well know how to shoot Skeet, but who have suddenly become worried into thinking too much about the station-8 targets, with the result that they are missing them rather consistently. Also, I might add that I have repeatedly tried this on good shots—men whom I knew were good field shots, but who just would not believe that they were capable of shooting fast enough to catch the station-8 targets when shooting from the regulation position at station 8.

To such shooters (and also to the beginner who shows aptitude, though slight lack of courage) I advance the shooter from station 8 *toward* the hi-trap—thus making the duration of shooting time even shorter!

Normally, of course, the shooter stands at station 8, 20 yards from the trap opening. By moving the shooter up to 19 yards, suddenly he is faced with the necessity of *forcing* himself to shoot faster—or shooting out of bounds—or shooting not at all. If the shooter still shows inclination here to be sluggish in his gun-handling and piddling with his aiming, I advance him still another yard closer to the hi-trap house— thus giving him only an "18-yard" shooting interval.

One excellent field shot, who beseeched me one week-end to help him with his station-8 targets, I actually advanced four yards before he began shooting in really snap timing and breaking his target cleanly. At last he got himself grooved into correct automatic functioning for this shot.

As soon as the shooter begins breaking his targets at the closer range, this of course is the signal that the cure has been effected—whereupon the coach should bring the shooter back to regulation range at station 8 and insist on his employing the same method of gun-handling and timing. It is sometimes startling what this course of training will do for

[164]

a good game shot who, unfamiliar with Skeet, seriously questions his ability to shoot in such fast time as he imagines is required on the station-8 targets.

Of course, in applying this rule it is well to know your man, too. If he is middle-aged, or past middle-age, you can be fairly certain that his vision is slow in accommodation. Understanding this, you will explain it patiently to him and tell him that he must then depend on the trained and subconscious pointing skill of his hands, rather than to try to make the station-8 shot a deliberately swung-on, aimed and methodically-led shot. Understand the shooter's equipment as thoroughly as you can. If you are a good coach you will sense his personal problem without too much delay.

In general, this system works out very successfully—of taking the young and inexperienced shotgun shooter back, so that he has a longer time to shoot on the station-8 target; then steadily advancing him nearer and nearer to regulation station-8 shooting range. Oppositely, in the case of the experienced shotgun shooter who simply hasn't gained (or who may have momentarily lost) confidence in his ability to break these two targets—here you adopt reverse tactics by advancing him from regulation position to shorter range, up nearer the trap house. The system, of course, applies to both station-8 targets, hi-trap and lo-trap.

20

CONCLUSION

~~~~~~

AT this concluding point, may I add that I have deliberately avoided making recommendations "wire-edged" in this book, with over-abundance of specific detail. I have tried to exclude too much detail in connection with *one* shooter's personal reactions on the Skeet field. I have tried to give only broad general principles that are fundamental. To go beyond this—to give minute details of personal experience and reactions—might serve mostly to confuse the reader. Such detail, after all, only narrowly reflects a single (and perhaps not at all average) individual's personal idiosyncrasies.

On the other hand, certain exceptions to this rule will be noted. The chapter on the eyes offers an example. On the subject of vision as a vital part of the shooter's equipment, I have purposely included certain information regarding personal peculiarities—simply because I feel that too little is generally known, even today, with reference to the tremendous effect that certain well-recognized peculiarities and deficiencies in vision may have on the wing shot's ultimate skill.

In the main, however, what has been given the reader in the foregoing chapters should be readily assimilable by the beginner without too much groping for correct interpretation and application of the author's meaning. I have included for the most part only basic fundamentals which should apply to all shooters.

[166]

CONCLUSION

Hold fast in particular to the suggestions made relative to the *Minimove Method*. This system of pivotal control is the most important contribution of this book. The system is easy to understand, elementary, and should not be difficult eventually to make a part of yourself.

Strictly speaking, of course, the *Minimove Method* is nothing new. It is merely that I bring to your attention a basic wing shooting principle, put it under a laboratory microscope and magnify it for you to see in closer detail; then, as an added touch, I give it a convenient and easily-remembered descriptive label. But the *Minimove Method* itself has long been in use by first-class wing shots.

Every outstanding wing shot, whether he is aware of it or not, "naturally" makes use of the principle of the *Minimove Method*. Every outstanding wing shot interprets and employs—though each in his own natural and perhaps unaware way—the fundamentals of pivotal control as outlined in the *Minimove Method*.

The principle is universal. How each shooter applies it to his own personal mental and physical make-up, however, is something for him alone to discover and develop patiently. So long as the gunner clearly understands this principle he cannot go wrong.

Now that you have learned to recognize the signs—and the *why* and *wherefore*—you will doubtless see good shots on the Skeet field actually applying the *Minimove* system of pivotal control from varying interpretations of correct stance. There will be those shooters who apply the principle with feet set rather widely apart. Such shooters will be those who have done much field shooting, possibly behind a spaniel, and who therefore appear all set for and in anticipation of the flush; also, those who adapt stance to the need for securing added leverage-control in handling heavy gun-weight.

Such shooters' application of the *Minimove* principle to their wide-spaced stance will be found usually correct—for them. Shooters may naturally apply the principle to their own particular physical and mental set-ups because the principle itself is natural and rational.

You will also see the *Minimove Method* used by good shots who keep their feet fairly close together; also, perhaps by equally good shots who slightly bend both legs at the knees in a sort of half-crouch, which in no way prevents them from employing the pivotal weight-shift so necessary to automatic, free-swinging follow-through.

In a nutshell, the *Minimove Method* simply induces automatic, free-swinging follow-through. Such sub-conscious and automatic follow-through is not a trick for the cerebral part of the brain to accomplish. As a matter of fact, the finished shooting function is much more deeply grounded in the sub-conscious than in the "upper stories" of the human brain.

In coincidence with our plan of avoiding intricacy of detail, we also purposely avoid offering the shooter any specific instruction on the doubles shooting at stations 1, 2, 6 and 7. After all, application of the principle of the *Minimove Method* in the doubles shooting is identical with the singles shooting. However, shooters will be forced to do considerable practicing here—rehearsing the "act" repeatedly in three to four minute intervals in "dry" practice—the better to groove their weight and muscles to the proper "feel" for the necessary swift *reversal of pivotal weight-shift* on the doubles pair—as, for example, on the right-quartering outgoer and left-quartering incomer in the doubles pair at station 2.

It is scarcely necessary to go into the matter in greater detail. To do so might be confusing to the reader, rather than helpful.

In fact, Article I in the credo of the wing shot might well read: *I believe that all men are created free and unequal.* The "free" is a technicality. The "unequal" is an actuality. Each of us is an individual—and though all of us are cast in

the same general mould, we are as unlike as peas in a pod—
and quite regardless of how much alike these well-known
vegetables may appear to the casual and careless observer.

Here's an example of how one man, relying too closely
on conclusions derived from his own personal experience,
might easily mislead the beginner: As a right-handed wing
shot I turn my left shoulder too much into the line of fire.
I know this is incorrect. Just the same, it enables me to wing-
shoot better. Should I advise others to do the same? Emphatically no! This habit of putting my left shoulder almost into
the line of fire was naturally induced when I changed over to
binocular shooting from the *right* shoulder, but with *left*
master eye.

Obviously, my shooting mechanism struggled to bring the
left eye into closer alignment over the barrel rib. Actually,
this was never quite accomplished. The aiming rib on my
shotgun was pushed in farther toward the middle of my face.
Or, rather, it was the other way around and I pressed my
face across the rearward prolongation of the sighting line
and thus effected a sort of "optical balance" between the two
eyes—neither eye aligning exactly over the rib, yet with gun
pointed more or less accurately by a sort of "welded" and
combined line of two-eyed vision.

As near as I can state it, this was accomplished by pressing
the gun inward, to the left of my right eye, about one-third
of the distance between the two eyes. Thus the master left
eye was apparently strong enough to function (in balance)
twice as far away from center of alignment as was the sub-
servient right eye.

Thus I do the thing wrong in my shooting. Yet it happens
to be *right* for me. But you can see how easy it is to advise
wrongly in this wingshooting game if one should fall into
the habit of generalizing from his own limited (and perhaps
quite unaverage) experience.

As another example of innocent and well-intentioned mis-

[169]

direction, take the following: One of my good friends in the pistol-shooting game—who happens to be not only one of the finest pistol shots in the United States, but who also writes most interestingly and intelligently on the subject—has several times put himself on record as believing that *the* correct stance (for everyone) in handgun shooting is for the shooter to face his target squarely—that is, for the shooter to have the line of his shoulders approximately at right angles to the line of fire.

This square-faced stance must be correct for my friend, because his skill with the handgun is of such superlative quality that he is easily entitled to place among the first five pistol shots in the country—and there are those who would accord him first place without much hesitation. But in advising everybody else to "do as I do," this great shot might seriously interfere with the development of an embryo handgun enthusiast, here and there, who didn't happen to be put together quite the same as he.

For example, I couldn't possibly use his recommendation. I shoot the handgun preferably from the right hand, with both eyes open, and aim with the left master eye—therefore turn my body almost directly into the line of fire in order to bring the left eye into alignment over the sights without tilting the head.

If I were pretty much alone in this oddity I wouldn't bother to raise the issue; but my good friend Mr. Milford Baker of Philadelphia, well-known pistol shot of Olympic rating, takes the same stance I do—in fact, aims exactly as I do, except that he closes the right eye. As another example, Mr. Ray Holland, Editor of *Field & Stream*, also shoots the handgun from the right hand, with both eyes open, and aims with the left eye—the same as I do—and also stands as I do.

The foregoing instances are mentioned only to illustrate the pitfalls the shooting writer may unwittingly step into—and all with the best of intentions—when he attempts to generalize from his own specific (and, of necessity, somewhat narrow) experience.

In conclusion, I urge the reader to hold fast to fundamental principles only in the initial stage of his development. Don't try to remember or to assimilate too much at once. Bear in mind that the thinking part of the brain has little to do with the finished shooting mechanism. You can't just "remember" to do it right. You have to do it right and keep on doing it right in sufficient repetition to make the cycle of action, reaction and coordination a part of yourself.

Re-read certain chapters when you are struggling with a certain type of shot, or with a particular problem. Study the illustrations throughout the book. Note, also, that the "don't" type of illustration is excluded. I have always felt that there are too vast a number of *right* things for the young shooter to learn, to clutter up his mind with wrong pictures of how *not* to do them.

Thus do we reach the end of the road. This is as far as I go—so good luck!

1. *Loaded Guns on the Field:* No loaded gun shall be allowed on the field except in the hands of the shooter and when he is in position to shoot.
2. *Number of Shells in the Gun:* During the shooting of single targets the shooter shall put but one shell in his gun at a time, with the exception that in registered shoots the management may permit the loading of two shells at any station, except Station 8, providing said management assumes full responsibility for the exercising of this exception; but the management cannot compel the loading of two shells in the shooting of singles. More than two shells shall not be put in the gun at any time.
3. *The Shooting Position:* When the shooter is ready to shoot he shall take his position at the shooting station with his gun in an informal shooting position, and shall not raise his gun to his shoulder to shoot until the target is seen in the air.

    The informal shooting position shall be defined as one in which the referee, standing at least ten feet directly to the side of the shooter from which he shoots, can see some part of the stock of the gun below or behind any part of the shooter's arm; and one in which no part of the stock of the gun shall be closer to the shoulder of the shooter than the width of the referee's hand.

    Shoulder in this connection is construed to mean that area covered by the butt of the gun when the gun is in actual shooting position.

[172]

The shooter shall then order a target, which shall be released by the puller any time after the order is heard within an indefinite period not to exceed three seconds. The referee shall delay and test the shooting position of any shooter about whom he is in question, and shall count any target as "no bird" when the shooter's position is not according to rule when target appears.

4. *Shooting Procedure:* The squad shall start shooting singles at Station 1 in the order that the names appear on the score sheet, and shall proceed through the singles at the stations as numbered, shooting the high house target first and the low house target second. Double shall be shot at Stations 1, 2, 6 and 7 in that order. In shooting singles each shooter shall shoot at both targets before leaving the station.

5. *Squad Position:* No member of a squad shall advance from the squad box toward the shooting station until it is his turn to shoot, and until the previous shooter has left the station. No member of a squad, having shot at a station, shall proceed toward the next station in such a way as to interfere with another shooter. The referee may warn or disqualify any member of a squad who violates this rule. No shooter shall order any target or shoot at any target except when it is his turn, or unless he has been given permission to shoot out of his regular turn by the referee. The result of any shooting done out of regular or approved turn shall not be recorded on the score, which shall be determined by the shooter shooting in his regular or approved turn.

6. *Regulation Targets:* A regulation target is one that appears after the shooter's call and within an indefinite period not to exceed three seconds, and which passes over a point which is in direct line with Stations 4 and 8, and six yards outside Station 8. This target, in still air, must pass within three feet of a spot fifteen feet vertically

over this point and carry to a distance equivalent, on level ground, to 55 to 60 yards from the traphouse from which it was thrown.

7. *Position at Station 8:* When shooting from Station 8, the shooter must stand near enough to the station marker so that his forward hand will be over the station. At Station 8 the entire squad will line up directly behind the shooter and shoot at targets from one trap in succession, before any member of the squad shoots at targets from the opposite traphouse.

8. *Irregular or Broken Targets:* Should an irregular or broken target be thrown in singles, the referee shall declare "no bird," and the single shall be thrown over again. Should two targets be thrown when singles are called for, the referee shall declare "no bird," and the single thrown over.

9. *Dead and Lost Targets:* Before declaring a target dead, the referee shall see a piece broken from the target while in regulation flight. Dusted targets shall not be counted as hits, nor shall perforated targets that are not retrieved after landing. Any shooter who neglects to have his gun ready when ordering a target or targets is not entitled to another shot, and the target or targets should be declared lost. A regular target that is not shot at after being ordered by the shooter, for other reasons than gun or ammunition failure, or for any reason being deemed adequate by the referee, shall be scored as a loss and the shooter shall proceed with the next shot in the regular program. However, in case of misfire or failure of the gun to operate through no direct fault of the shooter, he is entitled to another shot; but after two successive malfunctions the next target shall be declared lost if the gun fails to function; or after three malfunctions in one round any target not shot at during the remainder of

the round because of gun or ammunition failure shall be declared lost.

. *Interference:* It shall be the duty of the referee to see that each shooter has a fair opportunity to shoot in his turn, and should the referee decide that a shooter has been unduly interfered with while shooting, the referee may declare "no bird" and permit the shooter another shot. No claim of interference will be allowed by the shooter because of the appearance of a target from an adjoining field coming within his range of vision.

. *Shooting Bounds:* No hits shall be counted after the target from either trap has passed a point 42 yards from the traphouse from which it was thrown. When shooting at Station 8 no hits shall be counted after the target has passed over a point in direct line with Stations 4 and 8.

. *The Repeat Shot:* The first shot lost by the shooter in each round shall be repeated immediately. Should the first shot lost by the shooter in each round occur in a double, the lost target shall be repeated as a single, with the result of this shot counting on the score. Should the individual shooter break the first twenty-four targets of the regular round, and therefore be uncompelled to take a repeat shot up to that point, he may have his choice of trap and station for his twenty-fifth shot.

. *The Shooting of Doubles:* Unless the shooter about to shoot announces to the referee that he will shoot at the incoming target of the double first, and the outgoing target second, the outgoing target shall be shot at first, and the incoming target second. If the shooter in shooting doubles violates Rule 3 (Shooting Position) on the first target, the referee shall declare "no bird." A regulation double consists of two regulation targets thrown simultaneously.

[175]

PROOF DOUBLES

14. If in the shooting of doubles, the shooter breaks both targets of any double with his first shot, he shall be given a proof double. The hit on the first target of the original double shall be added to the result of his second shot of the proof double.

15. If in the shooting of doubles, a fragment of his first target properly broken, collides with and breaks the second target before the second shot is fired, this shall be considered the same as breaking both targets with one shot.

16. If the shooter shooting at a regulation double misses the first target and the two targets collide after the shot is fired, the shooter will be scored with a miss on the first target, and be given a proof double to establish a score on the second target.

17. If the shooter breaks the wrong or incoming target with his first shot at any double, he shall be given a lost bird on that shot, and shall be given a proof double. The results of the second shot only of the proof double shall be added to the loss of his first target on the original double.

18. If the shooter is thrown a broken target on his first or outgoing target of any double, it shall be declared "no bird," and he shall be given a proof double which shall determine his score.

19. If the shooter is thrown a broken or irregular target for his second or incoming target of any double, he shall be given a proof double which will determine his score with the proviso that if he shot at the original double the result of his first shot only shall be added to the result of his second shot of the proof double.

20. There shall be no penalty if a shooter refuses a double when either target is thrown broken or irregular in flight.

21. In case of gun failure after the first shot at any double, the shooter shall be given a proof double. The result of his shot at the original double shall be added to the result of his second shot on the proof double.

22. In doubles shooting, should the gun double on the first shot, the second shot shall be considered a malfunction and a proof double should be shot to determine the result of the second shot, providing there have not been three previous malfunctions in the round, or that such malfunction is not the third in succession.

23. *Note:* In all proof doubles, the shooter shall shoot two shots under regular doubles conditions. If the shooter shooting a proof double to establish a score on the incoming target should break both birds with one shot, or hit the incoming target with his first shot, or for any other reason beyond his control be unable to complete his proof double, he shall be given another proof double.

4. *Official Scores:* No scores or records shall be recognized as official unless the grounds are laid out according to specifications, and targets are regulation, and unless these rules are adhered to, or any special variation from them has been approved in writing by the National Skeet Shooting Association.

Printed in the United States
67328LVS00005B/108